Patent and Trademark Tactics and Practice

Patent and Trademark Tactics and Practice

Second Edition

DAVID A. BURGE

Registered Patent Attorney
David A. Burge Co., L.P.A.
Cleveland, Ohio

A Wiley-Interscience Publication

JOHN WILEY & SONS

New York · Chichester · Brisbane · Toronto · Singapore

Library of Congress Cataloging in Publication Data:

Burge, David A., 1943-
   Patent and trademark tactics and practice.

   "A Wiley-Interscience publication."
   Includes index.
   1. Patent practice—United States. 2. Patent laws and
legislation—United States. 3. Trademarks—United
States. I. Title.
KF3120.B87 1984   346.7304'86   84-2408
ISBN 0-471-80471-1   347.306486

Printed in the United States of America

10 9 8 7 6 5 4 3 2 1

To my wife Carolyn
The reasons increase day by day

Preface

I have tried to write a readable book from the viewpoint of a registered patent attorney who enjoys an active patent and trademark practice. My intention is to outline fundamental principles that should be understood by inventors and businesspersons engaged in the development, protection, and management of intellectual property. An effort has been made to avoid dwelling on complex legal issues and, instead, to concentrate on points of practical importance.

This book began as a checklist of points to cover with new clients. As the list grew, it provided an outline for much of the first edition. This second edition brings the book up to date both by treating new developments in the practice of intellectual property law and by treating areas of practice which increasingly are of interest and importance, such as biotechnology and computerware, where decisions of landmark importance have properly enhanced the definition of patentable subject matter.

Four years ago when this work was first published, the Patent and Trademark Office had practically nothing to speak of in the way of word processing equipment; since then, the Office has taken delivery of IBM's largest shipment ever of Displaywriter word processing equipment, whereby all handwritten examiner opinions have been eliminated for the first time in the history of the Office. Four years ago a steady stream of conflicting decisions was issuing from the various Circuit Courts of Appeal; now the new Court of Appeals for the Federal Circuit has been established to hear all patent appeals and to apply the patent law with uniformity. These are but a few of the many changes that continue to reshape the practice of intellectual property law.

It is not my purpose or intention to render legal advice or opinion in general terms for application to any particular situation. No general rules can be formulated for the solution of all intellectual property problems. Moreover, the law relating to intellectual property is continually growing and developing. Just as technology is developing at an escalating pace, so is the law that deals with it. Readers who have specific problems are urged to consult a registered patent practitioner for guidance.

While this book is intended chiefly for those whose skills and training lie in various fields of technology, I hope that it may also be of value to members of the bench and the bar whose practices are not regularly in the field of intellectual property law, but who may, on occasion, be called on to consider a question relating to intellectual property.

Since the majority of those who have deaings with registered patent attorneys are interested primarily in patents and trademarks as opposed to copyrights and other forms of intellectual property, the primary focus of this book is on patents and trademarks. I am indebted to those who have kindly offered suggestions for improving the content of that which follows. Any errors are my own.

DAVID A. BURGE

Cleveland, Ohio
February 1984

Contents

PART ONE   THE PATENT ATTORNEY'S BAILIWICK

Chapter 1   The Panorama of Intellectual Property   3

1-1	Interrelated Areas of Practice	3
1-2	Governmental Agencies Involved	5
1-3	Utility Patents	7
1-4	Design Patents	8
1-5	Plant Patents	10
1-6	Trademarks	10
1-7	Trade Names and Fictitious Names	11
1-8	Copyrights	11
1-9	Trade Secrets	12
1-10	Know–How and Show–How	12
1-11	Other Forms of Intellectual Property	12

Chapter 2   Working with a Patent Attorney   14

2-1	Don't Reinvent the Wheel	14
2-2	The Patent and Trademark Office as a Library	14
2-3	Searching as a Team Effort	16
2-4	Communicating the Total Picture	17
2-5	Avoiding Detrimental Delay	17
2-6	Typical Services	18
2-7	Choosing a Patent Attorney	19
2-8	Use of In–House Counsel	21

PART TWO   PATENTS

Chapter 3   Basic Features of Patents and Patent Systems   25

3-1	A Patent Viewed as a Contract	25
3-2	Grant Misconceptions	25
3-3	Monopoly Misconceptions	26
3-4	Humanitarian Misconceptions	26
3-5	A Negative Right	27
3-6	Why Are Patents Obtained?	29
3-7	The Value of a Patent	31
3-8	Benefits of a Patent System	32

Chapter 4   What Can Be Patented and By Whom   33

4-1	Ideas, Inventions, and Patentable Inventions	33
4-2	The Requirement of Statutory Subject Matter	34
4-3	The Requirement of Originality of Inventorship	37
4-4	The Requirement of Novelty	38
4-5	The Requirement of Utility	41
4-6	The Requirement of Nonobviousness	41
4-7	Statutory Bar Requirements	44

Chapter 5   Preparing to Apply for a Patent   46

5-1	The Patentability Search	46
5-2	Putting the Invention in Proper Perspective	47
5-3	Preparing the Application	48
5-4	Enablement, Best Mode, Description, and Distinctness Requirements	50
5-5	Functional Language in Claims	51
5-6	Product–by–Process Claims	52
5-7	Claim Format	52

5-8   Executing the Application   53
5-9   Patent and Trademark Office Fees   54
5-10 Small Entity Status   56
5-11 Express Mail Filing   57

Chapter 6   Prosecuting a Pending Patent Application   58

6-1   Patent Pending   58
6-2   Secrecy of Pending Applications   59
6-3   Duty of Candor   59
6-4   Initial Review of Application   60
6-5   Response to Office Action   62
6-6   Reexamination Following a Response   63
6-7   Interviewing the Examiner   65
6-8   Restriction and Election Requirements   65
6-9   Double Patenting Rejections   66
6-10 Patent Issuance   67
6-11 Safeguarding the Original Patent Document   68
6-12 Continuation, Division, and Continuation–in–
      Part Applications   68
6-13 Maintaining a Chain of Pending Applications   69

Chapter 7   Using an Issued Patent   70

7-1   The Need for Early Notice of Infringement   70
7-2   Patent Marking   70
7-3   False Marking   71
7-4   Correction of Defects Through Reissue   71
7-5   Reexamination Through Reissue   72
7-6   Protest   73
7-7   Statutory Disclaimer   73
7-8   Enforcing Patents Against Infringers   74
7-9   Defenses to Patent Enforcement   76
7-10 Uniformity in Patent-Related Decisions   77
7-11 Outcome of a Suit   78

7-12 Settling a Suit   78
7-13 Declaratory Judgment Actions   79
7-14 Failure to Sue Infringers   79
7-15 Voluntary Arbitration   80
7-16 Interferences   80

Chapter 8   Maintaining Proper Invention Records   82

8-1 Documenting Conception   82
8-2 The Need for Witnesses   82
8-3 Disclosure Format   83
8-4 Use of Invention Notebooks   83
8-5 Preparing a Disclosure for a Patent Attorney   85
8-6 Documenting Diligence   86

Chapter 9   Planning a Patent Program   88

9-1 Knowing the Prior Art   88
9-2 Keeping Abreast of the Patent Activities of Others   88
9-3 Avoiding Infringement   89
9-4 Protecting One's Own Developments   91
9-5 Encouraging Employee Development Contributions   92
9-6 Guarding Confidential Information   92

Chapter 10   Disclosing an Idea and Invention Marketing   95

10-1 Preparing to Seek Assistance   95
10-2 Submitting an Idea to a Manufacturer   96
10-3 Invention Marketing Firms   98
10-4 Disclosure Documents   100

Chapter 11   Assignments, Shoprights, and Licenses   102

11-1 Assignments in General   102
11-2 Employee Agreement Assigning Invention Rights   103

11-3	Prosecution of Application by Assignee	104
11-4	Issuance of Assigned Patent to Assignee	105
11-5	Shoprights	105
11-6	Licenses in General	105
11-7	Licenses and the Antitrust Laws	106
11-8	Typical License Provisions	107
11-9	Covenants Not to Sue	108

Chapter 12   Patent Protections Available Abroad   109

12-1	Canadian Filing	109
12-2	Foreign Filing in Other Countries	109
12-3	Annual Maintenance Taxes and Working Requirements	110
12-4	Filing Under International Convention	110
12-5	Filing on a Country–by–Country Basis	111
12-6	The Patent Cooperation Treaty	111
12-7	The European Patent Convention	112
12-8	Advantages and Disadvantages of International Filing	113
12-9	Trends in International Patent Protection	114

PART THREE   TRADEMARKS

Chapter 13   Basic Features of Trademarks   117

13-1	Relationship to Unfair Competition	117
13-2	Relationship to Monopolies	117
13-3	Relationship to Patents	119
13-4	Relationship to Copyrights	119
13-5	Relationship to Trade Names	120
13-6	Types of Trademarks	120
13-7	A Symbol of Goodwill	120

13-8   Eligible Subject Matter   121
13-9   The Essential Element: Use   122

        Chapter 14   Selection and Proper Use of Trademarks 123

14-1   The Foremost Rule   123
14-2   Protection Scope Depends on Character of Mark   124
14-3   Avoiding Abandonment   126
14-4   Selecting a Good Trademark   126
14-5   Proper Trademark Use   126
14-6   Utilizing Trademark Rights to Prevent the
        Marketing by Others of Look–Alike Products   128
14-7   Markings in Compliance with Federal Law   130
14-8   Prepublication Review and Maintaining
        Specimen Files   131

        Chapter 15   Trademark Registration   133

15-1   Eligibility for Federal Registration   133
15-2   Categories of Federal Registration   134
15-3   State Registration   135
15-4   Registration Procedure   136
15-5   Patent and Trademark Office Procedure   136
15-6   Maintaining a Registration in Force   138

        **Chapter 16   Assigning, Licensing, and Enforcing
                       Trademark Rights   140**

16-1   Trademark Assignments   140
16-2   Trademark Licensing   141
16-3   Trademark Infringement   141

PART FOUR   OTHER FORMS OF
INTELLECTUAL PROPERTY

Chapter 17   Design Patents   145

17-1	The Requirement of Ornamentality	145
17-2	Novelty and Nonobviousness Requirements	145
17-3	Embodiment in an Article of Manufacture	146
17-4	Application Content	146
17-5	Patent and Trademark Office Procedure	147
17-6	Infringement and Enforcement	147
17-7	Design Patent and Copyright Law Overlap	147
17-8	Design Patent and Trademark Law Overlap	148

Chapter 18   Plant Protection   150

18-1	Plant Patents	150
18-2	Certificates of Plant Variety Protection	151
18-3	Utility Patent Protection	151

Chapter 19   Copyrights   152

19-1	Comparison to Patents	152
19-2	Authorship, Originality, and Fixation Requirements	153
19-3	What Can Be Copyrighted	154
19-4	Registration Procedure	155
19-5	Term of Protection	156
19-6	Notice Requirement	157
19-7	Deposit Requirement	157
19-8	Features of the New Copyright Act	158
19-9	Benefits of Registration	159
19-10	Assignment of a Copyright	159

Chapter 20   Trade Secrets   160

20-1   The Nature of Trade Secrets   160
20-2   Relationship to Patents   161
20-3   Bases of Protection   162
20-4   Protecting the Secrecy of Trade Secrets   163
20-5   Employee Non–Competition Agreements   163

PART FIVE   PRESERVING AND PROTECTING
SPECIFIC TYPES OF INTELLECTUAL PROPERTY RIGHTS

Chapter 21   Computerware   167

21-1   What Is To Be Protected   167
21-2   Utility Patent Protection   168
21-3   Copyright Protection   168
21-4   Trade Secret Protection   169
21-5   Trademark Protection   170
21-6   Licensing   170
21-7   Copy Protection   170

Chapter 22   Biotechnology   172

22-1   Recognizing the Urgency   172
22-2   Available Types of Utility Patent Protection   173
22-3   Applying for Patent Protection   174
22-4   Foreign Patent Protection   174
22-5   Trade Secret Protection   174

Appendix 1   Typical Utility Patent   177

Appendix 2   Typical Design Patent   187

Appendix 3   Typical Trademark Registrations   191

Glossary   197

Index   201

PART ONE

THE PATENT ATTORNEY'S BAILIWICK

CHAPTER ONE

The Panorama of Intellectual Property

The concept of intellectual property is most easily understood through an overview of its domain. The term itself covers such a wide scope of personal property rights that it defies concise definition. Many traditional subjects such as patents, trademarks, and copyrights are included, as well as other forms of property of the intellect and some lesser-known subjects such as the right to publicity. This chapter provides an overview.

1-1 Interrelated Areas of Practice.   The bailiwick of the patent attorney, namely, the practice of intellectual property law, tends to be an area of mystery not only to those without formal legal training, but also to many members of the bench and bar. Even among businesspersons who must make decisions regarding the intellectual property assets they manage, it is rare to find an individual with a good understanding of how patents, trademarks, copyrights, trade secrets, and the like, interrelate.

During sessions spent with new clients, I have found that even those who have had considerable exposure to patent- and trademark-related matters often misconceive some very basic points. It is not uncommon for people to be puzzled by the different approaches that can be taken to protect various forms of intellectual property. Many have been misled by commonly held misconceptions that need to be dispelled.

Almost every patent attorney has encountered the situation in which a new client believes he has a "patent problem" when, in reali-

3

ty, a careful exploration of the facts discloses that the client has concerns ranging widely through several fields of intellectual property practice. Hopefully, much of the value a client obtains from consulting a patent attorney stems from the attorney's ability to determine not only which intellectual property concerns are present in the client's problem, but also how these concerns interrelate and the priorities with which they should be treated.

A factual situation narrated to me by a new client illustrates some of these interrelationships. The client had invented a new table game that used a foldable game board, an instruction sheet, some uniquely configured game pieces, and a novel timing mechanism. The game pieces needed to be able to snap together, but the client was having difficulty devising an appropriate snap-together connection. The client had a partner who was helping fund the development of the game, and these two individuals were operating their partnership using a name they had coined. A shortened version of the coined partnership name was expected to be used as a brand name for the new game. The client had developed the basic idea of the game during evening hours after work. He and his partner had collaborated in developing the unique configuration of the game pieces. The artwork for the game board had been created through the employment of an outside artist. The partnership was gearing up for production of the game and expected to be on the market within about three months. The "patent problem" the client wanted addressed was that of obtaining patent protection on the game "so that it would be fully protected when the partnership began marketing the game."

Readers with even a limited understanding of the various fields of intellectual property practice will readily appreciate that the foregoing situation raises concerns in several areas. Since the client was planning to go into production, a determination of whether the game infringed any existing patents was needed. The possibility of obtaining utility patent protection on the game itself and on the game's timing mechanism was a consideration, as was the possibility of obtaining design patent protection on the general layout of the game board and on the unique ornamental configuration of the game pieces. The issue of who owned copyright rights in the work created by the hired artist, and the desirability of taking suitable actions to preserve copyright rights with respect to such things as the game board artwork and the instruction pamphlet needed to be discussed. Determinations of whether the proposed brand name for the game infringed existing trademark rights and registrations of others, and of the registrability of the brand name as a trademark needed to be made. The desirability of conducting a state-of-the-art search on snap-together connections to assist the client in overcoming his remaining design obstacle presented yet another area for discussion.

Since state laws present both a trade name registration requirement and a local partnership name requirement, these matters needed to be treated. The questions of exactly who had invented what, and what entity would own the patent rights needed to be explored with respect to the pursuit of patent protection. The question of whether the client and/or his partner had employee agreements or had otherwise proceeded in a manner whereby their employers might have rights in their inventions also needed to be explored. Finally, the fact that intellectual property protections, particularly patents, sometimes take a substantial amount of time to obtain also needed to be considered.

In short, much of what follows in this book was unknown to the client. He clearly needed a crash course in the basics of intellectual property practice. Indeed, many clients who deal with patent attorneys also need a primer outlining the fundamentals of intellectual property practice. That is the purpose of this book.

1-2 Governmental Agencies Involved. The United States Patent and Trademark Office is responsible for the examination and the issuance of utility, design, and plant patents and federal trademark registrations.

The Patent and Trademark Office is a more far-reaching and complex operation than most people realize. Located in a series of interconnected buildings in the Crystal City community of Arlington, Virginia, just outside Washington, D.C., it is less than a five minute taxi ride from Washington National Airport. The annual budget of the Office is rapidly approaching $100 million. Approximately 3000 employees staff the Office, handling approximately 350,000 active cases and in excess of 20,000 new papers filed each day. The number of patent examiners is being increased and is projected to exceed 1400 by the end of fiscal year 1984.

Approximately 4½ million United States patent applications processed by the Office have matured into utility patents during the brief 200-plus years of existence of our country. Nearly 300,000 United States design patents and over 5000 plant patents have been issued, and over 1¼ million federal trademark registrations have been granted.

While pending applications are averaging about 24 months from filing to issue during 1983, the pendency time is expected to be cut to 18 months by 1987 as steps are being taken to automate and computerize the handling of pending cases. By 1985 the Office expects to diminish the time of pendency of trademark applications to as little as 13 months, with a first opinion on registrability being issued within 3 months of filing.

The Patent and Trademark Office also administers other programs. One is a Disclosure Document Program through which inventors can put on file disclosures of inventions they may subsequently want to patent. Another is a Defensive Publication Program that permits an applicant who is not interested in patenting an invention, but who does want to insure that no one else obtains a patent on its subject matter, to obtain what is called a Defensive Publication. This is achieved by waiving one's rights to an enforceable patent by consenting to the opening of the file of an application to public inspection, and by abandoning the pending patent application, whereupon an abstract of the case will be published by the Office.

The registration of copyrights is adminstered by a branch of the Library of Congress known as the Copyright Office. Of the more than 700,000 copies of works that are deposited annually to make registrations, over half are transmitted to the Library of Congress to enhance its collection. A thoroughly revised and revamped copyright act be-

came effective on January 1, 1978, streamlining copyright registration procedures and enhancing the scope of available protections.

The Department of Agriculture administers the issuance of certificates of plant variety protection in accordance with a statute enacted
in 1970, titled the Plant Variety Protection Act.

The secretaries of state of the 50 states administer state registrations of trademarks, trade names, and fictitious names. Several
jurisdictions have mandatory state and local name registration requirements.

No governmental agencies are charged with the regulation of other forms of intellectual property such as trade secrets, know-how,
show-how, and the right to publicity. These additional categories of
intellectual property are not ordinarily protected through the issuance of any sort of certificate by a government agency, but rather are
protected through federal, state, and local laws construed and enforced by the courts.

1-3 Utility Patents. When one speaks of obtaining a patent it is
ordinarily assumed that what is intended is a utility patent. This is
printed document issued by the United States Patent and Trademark
Office wherein the character of an invention is described in such detail as will enable one skilled in the art to which the invention pertains
to practice the invention, and wherein one or more claims are set
forth particularly pointing out and distinctly claiming the subject
matter for which protection has been obtained. A utility patent has a
term of 17 years measured not from the time when an application for a
patent was filed, but rather from the date on which the patent was
actually issued by the Patent and Trademark Office. A *utility patent* is
a grant of a *negative right* giving its owner the right to exclude others
from making, using, and/or selling the claimed invention. A utility
patent does not necessarily give to its owner the *positive right* to
make, use, and/or sell the claimed invention, as is brought out in
Chapter 3, particularly Section 3-4.

Utility patents are granted to protect new, useful, and unobvious
processes, machines, compositions of matter, and articles of manu-

facture. A comparison of some of the basic features of utility patents with those of design patents, trademarks, and copyrights is presented in Table 1. A further discussion of utility patents is in Part II of this book, with a sample utility patent provided in Appendix I.

Approximately 100,000 applications for utility patents are presently being filed each year in the United States, and approximately 75,000 utility patents are currently being issued annually. Despite the fact that utility patents are enforceable for only 17 years, about a fourth of the utility patents that have issued during the entire history of the United States are still in effect. More than a third of the utility patents being issued currently by our government are owned by foreign nationals. About three times as many patents are assigned to corporations as are retained in the hands of individual inventors.

Most foreign countries also have patent systems providing for the issuance of utility patents. Convention agreements entered into by various groups of countries have, in recent years, helped to reduce the relatively high costs and difficulties encountered in obtaining widespread patent protection abroad. There are significant differences among the patent laws of other nations with respect to such important factors as the terms of protection of patent grants, the degree to which patent applications are examined prior to issuance as patents, and requirements for periodically paying maintenance fees to keep patents in force. The subject of protecting an invention abroad is discussed in Chapter 12.

1-4 Design Patents.   Design patents cover new, original, ornamental, and unobvious designs for articles of manufacture. That is, a design patent covers the appearance of an object. During 1982, the law was changed to prescribe a 14 year term for design patents. Prior to this change, a design patent could have a term of $3\frac{1}{2}$, 7, or 14 years from its date of issuance, as elected by the patent owner prior to issuance. The owner of a design patent is granted the right to exclude others from making, using, or selling an article having the ornamental appearance shown in the drawing that forms a part of the issued design patent. Like the grant of a utility patent, the grant of a design patent is a *negative right,* as is explained more fully in Section 3-4.

Table 1 Comparison of Utility Patents, Design Patents, Trademarks, and Copyrights

	Utility Patent	Design Patent	Trademark	Copyright
Protectible subject matter	Useful processes, machines, articles of manufacture, and compositions of matter	Ornamental designs for articles of manufacture	Words, names, symbols, or other devices that serve to distinguish one's goods or services	Writings, music, works of art, and the like, that have been reduced to a tangible medium of expression
Sources of protection	Issuance of patent by the Patent and Trademark Office	Issuance of patent by the Patent and Trademark Office	Common law protection, so long as proper use continues State Registrations available Issuance of Federal Registration by the Patent and Trademark Office	Federal law protects once has been reduced to a tangible medium Enforceable only on issuance of Registration Certificate by Copyright Office
Terms of protection	17 years from issuance of patent	3½, 7, or 14 years, depending on term elected prior to issuance of patent	State terms vary Typically, 10 years and renewable 20 years from issuance of federal Registration, renewable for additional 20 year terms	Life of author, plus 50 years for works created after January 1, 1978
Tests for infringement	Making, using, or selling invention claimed in patent	Making, using, or selling design shown in patent drawings	Likelihood of confusion, mistake, or deception	Copying of protected subject matter

Many foreign countries do not provide for the protection of ornamental designs. In Canada, the Industrial Design Protection Act provides for a five year registration of ornamental designs applied to articles of manufacture. The original registration is renewable once to extend its term for another five years.

Design patents are treated in Chapter 17. A copy of a design patent is provided in Appendix II.

1-5   Plant Patents.   Plant patents are issued on new varieties of plants that have been asexually reproduced, with the exception of tuber-propagated plants and those found in an uncultivated state. Patentable plants must have been reproduced by means other than seeds, such as by the rooting of cuttings or by grafting. Plant patents have a term of 17 years measured from their dates of issuance.

Relatively few plant patents have been issued; the average in recent years is about 100. Few foreign countries provide for plant patent protection. The types of protections available for plants are presented in Chapter 18.

1-6   Trademarks.   The term "trademark" is commonly used in two different senses. In one, it refers to a wide variety of different types of commercial marks, including service, certification, and collective marks. In a more restricted sense, the term refers to a particular type of commercial mark that differs from service, collective, and certification marks. In other words, while the term "trademark" is commonly used interchangeably with the term "commercial mark," the latter is technically of broader scope than the former. While it would be more proper to refer to the various types of marks as "commercial marks," the several types of commercial marks are more commonly referred to by the catch-all term "trademarks." Indeed, even the name of the government agency handling the registration of commercial marks— the Patent and Trademark Office—uses "trademark" rather than "commercial mark."

Over 400,000 active registered trademarks are on the Principal Register of the Patent and Trademark Office. Trademark applications are now being received by the Office at a steadily increasing rate, which presently stands at about 60,000 per year. Unquestionably, trademarks are assuming greater significance in our society. They not only symbolize sources from which goods and services originate, but also act as assurance of quality. A product bearing a trademark known to be associated with goods of quality will command a higher price in the marketplace than will a lesser-known brand. As the franchising phenomenon has snowballed during recent years, trademark licensing has grown in importance.

Part III discusses trademarks, and copies of three trademark registrations are provided in Appendix III.

1-7 Trade Names and Fictitious Names. A *trade name* is the name or designation under which a person, partnership, corporation, firm, association, society, foundation, federation, organization, or the like, does business. A *fictitious name* is any name used in trade or business that does not fully identify the user.

Since a name one uses in business may qualify both as a trade name and as a fictitious name, those states having registration requirements for these types of names usually let the owner elect one or the other of the two categories for registration. Trade name registration usually gives more protection than fictitious name registration.

In many localities there are local registration requirements for partnership and unincorporated firm names. Federal registration of a business name is not permitted unless it is used in commerce as a trademark. The requirements that must be met to permit federal registration as a trademark are discussed in Chapter 15.

1-8 Copyrights. Copyright protection is available for original works of authorship that are fixed in any tangible medium of expression. The number of copyright registrations issued annually is growing steadily and is now in excess of 450,000.

Under the new Copyright Law, which took effect January 1, 1978, works created after this date may be protected for a term consisting of the life of the author, plus 50 years. If a work has been jointly authored, the term of protection endures for the life of the last surviving author, plus 50 years. Chapter 19 deals with copyrights and points out that obtaining a federally issued copyright registration is not essential to establish copyright rights in a work.

1-9   Trade Secrets.   A *trade secret* may consist of any formula, pattern, device or compilation of data used in one's business that gives one an economic advantage over competitors who do not know or use such information.

State laws and court decisions define the scope of protection available for trade secrets. While matters of general knowledge in an industry cannot be said to constitute trade secrets, an assemblage of individual pieces of previously known information that, taken together, gives one an economic benefit over competitors clearly can constitute a trade secret.

Trade secrets are discussed in Chapter 20.

1-10   Know-How and Show-How.   Some compilations of information are licensable simply because others are willing to pay for an organized presentation of the information they need to become established in a field where the owner of such know-how and show-how has expertise. Know-how tends to take the form of information that can be reduced to drawing and writing. Show-how involves information conveyed by demonstration.

Know-how and show-how are especially valuable in the licensing of technology in underdeveloped countries. One need not have patents or otherwise protectable information to reap a handsome return from the licensing of know-how and show-how. In many instances, the recipients of know-how and show-how might well be able to learn by other means all that they are taught by the entity paid to provide this information. Often, however, recipients are willing to pay simply to minimize the time and experimentation that would otherwise be required to assemble exactly the right combinations of information that satisfy their immediate needs.

1-11   Other Forms of Intellectual Property.   Several other forms of intellectual property are recognized in our country and abroad, with new forms appearing occasionally. An example of a form of protection not recognized in the United States but observed in some countries such as West Germany and Japan is the petty patent or utility model registration. An example of a relatively new form of intellectual property that has gained attention recently in this country is the right to publicity. First recognized in the early 1950s, it deals with an individual's right to control the use of such personal assets as his name and likeness for private or commercial gain.

CHAPTER TWO

Working with a Patent Attorney

Surprisingly little is known by the general public regarding the broad scope of services available through a registered patent attorney. This chapter offers some suggestions about when and how the assistance of patent counsel should be sought.

2-1 Don't Reinvent the Wheel. Many inventors make the mistake of investing months if not years of effort in developing an invention before contacting a patent attorney. The dismay some of these people express when a patentability search conducted by their attorney establishes beyond question that their inventions have been old in the art for decades is a spectacle to witness. Too many inventors devote their valuable time to reinventing the wheel. Far too few take proper advantage of patent searches to show them the current state of technology, to give them ideas they can use to further their efforts, and to guide them in directions where their inventions avoid infringement concerns.

2-2 The Patent and Trademark Office as a Library. The U.S. Patent and Trademark Office is probably the largest and best organized technological library in the world. It houses nearly 25 million documents representing what has been done previously, or the *prior art*. These documents, which will double in number by the year 2000, are divided for ready reference into approximately 100,000 technical subclasses. Documents are presently being added to this collection at the rate of about 600,000 per year.

A recent survey indicates that over 90 percent of the technology disclosed in patents is not disclosed elsewhere. Regardless of whether this survey is correct, it cannot be disputed that the Office constitutes an incredible repository of information presenting much opportunity to every technologically oriented individual. Yet, the percentage of inventors who take advantage of the unique compilation of information available to them in the United States Patent and Trademark Office is miniscule.

One summer during my college years, I worked in the engineering section of a production plant of one of the *Fortune* 500 companies. The engineering section had many fine engineers, but one among the group had developed a reputation for devising highly innovative solutions to longstanding problems. The promotions and raises he received reflected his stellar contributions. He was no genius, yet his abilities to successfully tackle difficult situations clearly was far above average. Some years later when I was working in the Public Search Room of the Patent and Trademark Office, I found this same fellow judiciously searching through patents that related to a new problem he had been asked to solve. Only then did he tell me the simple secret of his phenomenal success. Twice a year he spent a day or two of his vacation time searching patents to get ideas that would help him with his current projects. He was using the extraordinary library of the Patent and Trademark Office to stimulate his thinking, to point out proposed solutions that had been tried by others without success, and to zero in on approaches that presented good likelihoods of success. In the process he became aware of active patents that needed to be avoided to assure that his company did not encounter infringement concerns. He estimated the rewards he had received in the form of pay raises and bonuses resulting directly from the time he had spent doing search work in the Patent and Trademark Office to be about $15,000 per day of search time.

I have told this true tale many times with the result that several of my clients have visited the Public Search Room. I know none who have made a serious study of patents relating to their fields of interest that have failed to benefit from the effort.

2-3   Searching as a Team Effort.   In my own practice, I have occasionally found it desirable to take an inventor with me to Washington and work together in conducting a search. While members of the public are not required to have a registered patent attorney accompany them to the Patent and Trademark Office to conduct searches, those who are unfamiliar with the operations of the Office can benefit from having readily at hand the assistance of an experienced searcher.

An experienced searcher can help locate certain bodies of art that are unavailable in the Public Search Room and can help decipher the classification system used by the Office. He knows how to thread through the maze of the several buildings that house the Patent and Trademark Office and contact examiners (PTO personnel who handle the examination of patent applications) to obtain their assistance in laying out a proper field of search. An experienced searcher can teach an inexperienced one techniques for quickly scanning patent copies to evaluate their possible pertinence. He can also help with other fundamental prerequisites that will further an inventor's efforts to cover a maximum field of search with a minimal time investment.

Similarly, an inventor can assist a patent attorney in the performance of a search by bringing to this effort his understanding of the full spectrum of inventive approaches he has been considering. The inventor is therefore capable of recognizing patents that the average searcher might not know would be of interest to the inventor. Still another advantage that results when an inventor participates in a search effort is that the inventor becomes cognizant of the degree of inventive activity currently being enjoyed by the particular field of art in which he has an interest. An inventor can readily see the names of individuals and companies most active in the area of interest and can often recognize inappropriate inventive approaches taken by his peers. An inventor or other technical person well-versed in the areas of development that interest a company is in a unique position to gain a maximum of information by participating in a search effort.

Within a decade the Patent and Trademark Office will be moving toward totally paperless search files. At the present time, about 7% of the 25 million documents that have been acquired for the search files of the Office are missing or misfiled. As a pilot paperless Public Search Room is established, the search files will achieve 100% integrity. As search facilities are expanded, direct access to the search file data base through telecommunications will become a reality. In short, the fabulous library of the Public Search Room is not far away from going on-line with the world.

2-4   Communicating the Total Picture.   In order for a patent attorney to serve a client properly, it is important that the attorney understand certain fundamentals of a client's business. It is equally essential that the client understand certain fundamentals of intellectual property practice so the client can make productive and efficient use of the patent counsel. If a significant development effort is being undertaken and a substantial number of solution approaches are being considered, the character of the overall effort should be communicated to one's patent attorney. When an inventor fails to advise the patent counsel of the total picture, the attorney tends to view this limited information as the only area of the inventor's interest. In performing patentability, state-of-the-art, and/or infringement studies regarding a particular development, the attorney may unknowingly pass over and fail to report to the inventor substantial additional information that could have great bearing on the overall effort.

While the client's present needs may be confined to an isolated area of the client's overall activity, it often occurs that the patent attorney's work is of much greater benefit to the client if the attorney has first been permitted to view the isolated area in proper perspective with regard to the client's other activities. This simple truth ought to be so self-evident that it need not merit inclusion in print, but it is so commonly and detrimentally ignored by clients seeking to minimize their patent counsel's time expenditure that its importance needs to be emphasized.

2-5   Avoiding Detrimental Delay.   Far too many inventors delay, to their detriment, contacting a patent attorney until long after they have made inventions they believe are entitled to protection. In many instances the services of a patent attorney could prevent the loss of patent rights. This can occur if one technically abandons or fails to diligently pursue an invention, or delays for an undue length of time in filing an appropriate patent application.

Some individual inventors take their inventions first to one of the many invention marketing companies and delay in meeting with a patent attorney until such time that there may be little a patent attorney can do to assist them in obtaining patent protection. Some of the problems inventors have been known to encounter in dealing with invention marketing companies are discussed in Chapter 10.

2-6 Typical Services.   Services commonly performed by competent, registered patent counsel include index and assignment searches to locate patents issued or assigned to a particular individual or company; state-of-the-art searches to ascertain what developments in a particular field of art are already known so that much trial-and-error experimentation by an inventor can be avoided; infringement studies to ascertain whether infringement concerns are involved in undertaking the manufacture of a new product or the performing of a new service; validity studies to determine whether a patent that appears to constitute an infringement concern is, in fact, enforceable; evaluation of patents, trademarks, and copyrights for purposes of purchase or sale; pursuing patent, trademark, or copyright protections in the United States and abroad; counseling the client on which types of protections are best to pursue; advising clients with regard to programs for protecting trade secrets and other fruits of their research and development programs; assisting clients in the enforcement of their intellectual property rights against others; advising clients regarding infringement claims asserted against them by third parties; assisting clients in the licensing and assigning of rights in their intellectual property; and a great many other related matters such as the recording of trade names and fictitious names used in business to comply with state statutes.

While it is true that one is not required to work with a registered patent practitioner to deal with the Patent and Trademark Office, and while some inventors are successful in preparing and prosecuting their own patent applications, I believe the probabilities of obtaining the broadest available protections and of avoiding pitfalls are greatly improved if one works through a competent, registered patent counsel.

Sometimes, however, not even an experienced patent attorney can help. When a client discloses a spaceship that flies "because it is lighter than air because it is made with aluminum screws," I confess that my background has not adequately prepared me to be of service. Every patent attorney gets a share of star-spangled nuts; the problem is, however, that many of our greatest inventors probably came across as funny farm residents during their first visit to a patent attorney.

2-7 Choosing a Patent Attorney. While the Patent and Trademark Office maintains a roster of attorneys and agents registered to practice before it, the Office is prohibited from assisting an inventor in choosing a patent practitioner. A roster titled *Directory of Registered Patent Attorneys and Agents Arranged by States and Counties* can be purchased from the Superintendent of Documents, United States Government Printing Office, Washington, D.C. 20402. A copy is available in the patent sections of the public libraries of many large cities. The difference between *attorneys* and *agents* is not one of technical training; both must have had appropriate technical training to secure registration. However, an attorney has attended law school and is a member of the bar of at least one state in addition to having fulfilled all of the requirements to be registered as a patent agent.

The practices of patent and trademark law are among the oldest of recognized legal specialties. Patent and trademark attorneys are permitted to list themselves in the yellow pages of telephone books under the headings "patent attorneys" and "trademark attorneys." Also many large cities have bar associations with referral services through which contact can be made with a patent attorney, usually at no cost or at only a nominal charge for an initial consultation.

In selecting a patent attorney, it is important that a client find someone he can trust because he must be able to talk openly and free-ly with his patent attorney. A mistake some clients make in selecting a patent attorney is to underestimate the amount of time they will spend with the attorney during coming years. While a client may en-vision a present need as requiring only the filing and prosecuting of a relatively simply patent application, as time goes by there are often improvements to be protected, license agreements to be negotiated, and infringement concerns to be dealt with. If one has selected an attorney he is uncomfortable with or who is not knowledgeable about handling the full range of the client's needs, the time may arise when the client will feel compelled to take his work elsewhere.

It is appropriate to ask about the attorney's understanding of the technology involved with the client's work. Patent attorneys have tra-ditionally tended to specialize in such general areas as mechanical, chemical, or electrical arts. Some patent attorneys further restrict their practices to limited segments of technology within these tradi-tional areas. While patent attorneys are accustomed to dealing with inventions of widely varying degrees of complexity and spanning very different fields of technology, if an attorney can be found who is well-versed in the technology that is of particular interest to the inventor, so much the better. Some technologies are so unique that no experi-enced counsel can be found who has a mastery of them. In such cases, more than the usual amount of time will need to be spent providing the attorney with the background needed to serve the client.

One caveat in searching for a practitioner knowledgeable in a par-ticular area of technology is that, once found, this person's expertise may well have developed through representation of the client's prin-cipal competitor. His present or even past representation of one's competitor may pose a conflict of interest that may prohibit him from representing others in the same field of technology.

The greatest concentration of patent attorneys in the country is in the general vicinity of Washington, D.C. Advantages obtained through working with a Washington attorney lie principally in the ease of access the Washington attorney has to the Patent and Trademark Office. Advantages gained from working with a patent attorney situated in one's own locality lie in the ease of access the client has to the patent counsel.

Since business with the Patent and Trademark Office if carried on largely in writing, many patent attorneys find no significant disadvantage in having their practice located several states removed from Washington. Many patent attorneys with practices removed from the Washington area make fairly regular trips there to interview examiners and participate in the conduct of important search work. As the operations of the Office become truly paperless, dealing with the Office increasingly will be conducted using telecommunication equipment and terminals, which will provide ease of access to the Office regardless of where counsel may reside.

2-8   Use of In-House Counsel.   As a company's business grows, it will pay the company to employ a full-time patent attorney who will oversee the handling of the company's intellectual property concerns. An in-house patent counsel can do much to coordinate the patent activities of a company and to keep abreast of the total picture of the company's developmental efforts. This practitioner can set up proper procedures for insuring that invention records are maintained and that disclosures meriting patent protection are given adequate consideration. He will see that patent applications are prepared and prosecuted either by his own staff or by outside counsel, that submitted ideas are handled in appropriate ways, and that the company's trademarks are used properly and are protected. He will assure that the company's trade secrets are guarded, that infringement concerns are treated properly, and will manage other intellectual property concerns. Usually responsibility for assuring that key employees sign agreements that define invention ownership rights and trade secret protection duties lies with in-house patent counsel.

An in-house patent counsel should not be expected to handle personally all the intellectual property activities of a company. Many situations will occur when he will consult outside experts (sometimes jokingly referred to as "out-house" counsel) about the handling of particularly involved matters, and certainly when handling matters that involve litigation.

REFERENCES

Buckles, Robert A., *Ideas, Inventions and Patents*, Wiley, New York, 1957.

Hoar, Roger S., *Patent Tactics and Law*, Ronald Press, New York, 1950.

Holmes, William C., *Intellectual Property and Antitrust Law*, Clark Boardman, New York, 1983.

Kile, Bradford E., "The Property Panorama," in *Concentrated Course in Intellectual Property Course Book*, Federal Publications, New York, 1978.

Kintner, Earl W., and Jack Lahr, *An Intellectual Property Law Primer*, Clark Boardman, New York, 2nd Ed., 1982.

PART TWO
PATENTS

CHAPTER THREE

Basic Features of Patents
and Patent Systems

The basic character of a patent and the reasons that all major countries have patent systems are widely misunderstood. Therefore, I will lay the foundation for the remainder of this book by explaining just what patent is and is not, and why a patent system is desirable.

3-1 A Patent Viewed as a Contract. A view of a patent that businesspersons appreciate is that it is a contract between the government and an inventor. In exchange for the inventor's disclosure of an invention previously unknown to the public, the government promises the inventor certain exclusive rights in the invention for a limited period of time. As a part of this contract, the inventor agrees to the government's publication of the invention upon expiration of the patent. During the time the patent contract is in force, the public has access to the published disclosure of the invention and can use its teachings in constructive thinking to forward the development of the art, whereby improvements are often promulgated. Members of the public may also approach the patent owner while the patent is in force seeking permission to practice the invention on terms suitable to the patent owner.

3-2 Grant Misconceptions. There are those who prefer to think of a patent as a grant—from a government to an individual—of exclusive rights in an invention in exchange for a disclosure of the invention to the public. A danger of viewing a patent as a grant is that it tends to be thought of as a gift from the government to an inventor.

To the contrary, an inventor of a patentable invention already has the exclusive, perpetual right to the invention and may enjoy this exclusive right forever by keeping his knowledge of the invention secret. By encouraging an inventor to make a full public disclosure in exchange for the right to exclude others from making, using, or selling the invention during a limited period of time, the government does not take from the public what it is already enjoying. Indeed, patents can only be issued on new developments not previously known or used.

3-3   Monopoly Misconceptions.   A very common misunderstanding associated with the grant of patent is the opinion that it confers a monopoly on an inventor. A patent so seldom grants a monopoly to an inventor that it is almost universally wrong to think of a patent as conferring monopoly rights. Patents covering inventions so basic that they preclude the viable existence of competitors in a particular field of practice are rare. A patent owner often will find that competitors are able to devise ways of performing substantially the same function that his invention serves without infringing his patent. While alternative approaches left open to competitors may be less desirable than the patented approach, it is very unusual for the issuance of a patent to actually give rise to a monopoly situation.

One's ownership of a patent does not constitute a monopoly any more than does one's ownership of an automobile. Both types of ownership constitute desirable rights in private property. Just as people can do what they want with their automobiles insofar as they do not cause unlawful injury to the rights of others, they should likewise be able to deal relatively unrestrictedly with their patent properties. Unfortunately, in recent years the antitrust laws of our country have been interpreted to encroach on patent owners' freedom, as is discussed in Chapter 11 under the subject of licensing.

3-4   Humanitarian Misconceptions.   Some so-called humanitarians raise the notion that, were it not for patents blocking the way of humanity's progress, we would all be faring better than we are today. This is nonsense.

Sir Alexander Fleming, the famed British bacteriologist who started the antibiotic age with his discovery of penicillin back in 1929 had exactly the same magnanimous idea. He decided against pursuing patent protection so that his discovery could be commercialized without hindrance, and be put into worldwide use as quickly as possible. The result of this fatal folly was that, without the shield of patent protection, no commercial manufacturers could be found who would make the investment needed to find a way to purify the drug and develop techniques needed for manufacture. In a nutshell, Fleming's humanitarian refusal to procure a patent was a major factor in delaying commercial production of penicillin for about 14 years until the era of World War II. Who knows how many tens of thousands of lives might have been saved by penicillin during those years of delay.

The simple fact is that patent protection truly does "promote the progress of science and useful arts." Refraining from pursuing patent protection seldom can be excused on humanitarian grounds.

3-5   A Negative Right.   Unquestionably the single most common misunderstanding about patents is the character of the right conferred by a patent grant. While the right of ownership in most personal property is a *positive right*, the right of ownership in a patent is a *negative right*. It is the negative right to exclude others from making, using, or selling the patented invention. A patent does *not* give the inventor the positive right to make, use, or sell his own invention, but rather grants to the inventor the negative right *to exclude others* from making, using, or selling the invention.

Whether an inventor may have received a patent on an invention has nothing to do with whether the inventor himself can make, use, or sell the invention. Indeed, in making, using, or selling his own invention, the inventor may find that he infringes the patent rights of others. This concept is so misunderstood that patent attorneys have come to use a fairly standard example in emphasizing the importance of this concept to their clients. I do not know the origin of the example that follows, but have come to refer to it in dealing with my own clients as "The Parable of the Chair."

The Parable of the Chair

Once upon a time, in a country far, far away, it was commonplace for citizens to rest their weary bones by sitting on logs and boulders. But logs and boulders tended to be damp and were difficult to move about when one wished to change his seating location. The need was clearly present for an improved seating appliance.

Having recognized this problem and given it careful study, Abraham took a small plank and affixed to its underside three depending legs. He experimented with his invention and found that it was stable and portable and constituted a considerable improvement over logs and boulders. He called this invention a stool. Since stools were previously unknown and since the country had a patent system, Abraham applied for and was successful in obtaining a patent on his platform with three legs.

Bartholomew bought one of Abraham's stools, but found it uncomfortable. The stool provided no support for his back and occasionally tipped over when he seated himself too close to one side of the platform. Bartholomew decided to add a fourth leg to the stool, an upstanding back, and two arms. He called the resulting improvement a chair. The chair was found to be far more comfortable than its three-legged predecessor and yet preserved the stool's lightweight, portable character. The Patent Office, in recognition of Bartholomew's contribution, granted a patent to Bartholomew on his chair.

And then along came Clyde. Clyde was a man of movement who did not care at all for things that stood still. Clyde considered the chair to constitute a dull and uninteresting development and decided that chairs would be vastly improved by the addition of curved base members to the undersides of their legs. Clyde called his improvement a rocking chair. And the Patent Office, recognizing the ingenuity of Clyde's contribution, granted a patent to Clyde on his rocking chair.

Now for the question of who has what rights. Since a patent gives one the negative right to *exclude others* from making, using, or selling his invention, Abraham can exclude all others from the practice of his stool invention; Bartholomew can exclude others from the practice of his chair invention; and Clyde can exclude others from the practice of his rocking chair invention. Moreover, since Abraham's patent is *basic* to the portable seating appliance art, he can make stools without fear of infringing Bartholomew's chair patent or Clyde's rocking chair patent. Because Abraham's invention is basic to the art, his patent not only confers the *negative* right to exclude others, but also, under these circumstances, effectively confers to Abraham the *positive* right to make, use, and sell his invention without any fear of infringing patent rights of others. But realize, *basic* inventions that can be practiced with no concern at all about infringing rights of others are rare.

Bartholomew is in a different position with regard to his proposed manufacture of chairs. While Bartholomew's patent will permit him to exclude others from making devices that include a platform with four legs, a back, and two arms, his patent does not necessarily give him the right to make these devices. Indeed, since a chair includes a platform and three legs (that is, the subject matter of Abraham's stool patent), chairs made by Bartholomew would infringe Abraham's patent. If Bartholomew undertakes the manufacture of chairs without first reaching a suitable agreement with Abraham, he should not be at all surprised to receive a cease and desist letter from Abraham's patent counsel.

Clyde has a similar, but greater, problem if he wants to manufacture rocking chairs. While Clyde can exclude others from making, using, and selling rocking chairs, the problem remains that a rocking chair includes not only a platform with four legs, a back, and two arms, but also a platform with three legs. In short, Clyde's proposed manufacture of rocking chairs would not only infringe Bartholomew's chair patent, but also Abraham's stool patent. It is therefore necessary that Clyde negotiate suitable agreements with both Abraham and Bartholomew.

If another citizen, Demetri, should desire to make rocking chairs, he would find himself in the very uncomfortable position of having to reach separate agreements with Abraham, Bartholomew, and Clyde. The fact that Demetri may obtain a further patent, for instance, a design patent on the attractive appearance of a particular type of rocking chair, does not confer on Demetri the right to make even the patented style of rocking chair he invented.

In short, because one may have a patent on an invention does not give that person the right to practice the invention. Patents enable their owners to *exclude others* from practicing their patented inventions. This exclusionary privilege, which forms the subject of a patent grant, is a negative right not a positive one. Only when the invention is very basic to the art does the grant of a patent take on characteristics of a positive right.

3-6 Why Are Patents Obtained? People obtain patents for many reasons. Almost every practicing patent attorney has encountered the situation of someone simply wanting a patent to frame and put on his living room wall to impress the neighbors. A patent sought for this purpose often is relatively easy to obtain because both the patent attorney and the inventor understand, from the outset, that the inventor does not care much about the scope of the invention protection included in the resulting patent, and claims of extremely narrow scope may therefore be pursued. Under these circumstances, the probability frequently favors one's succeeding in efforts to obtain at least some sort of extremely narrow patent protection.

Many people come to patent attorneys with little more than the rudimentary elements of a basic idea, seeking patent protection in the hope that they will be able to sell their patent-protected invention to a company that will pay the inventor significant royalties. The percentage of those individuals who succeed in efforts to use the patent system in this way is relatively small.

As Chapter 10 points out, many companies are reluctant to adopt an idea received from an outside inventor. If the idea has genuine merit, it is not uncommon for the company's research staff to already have the idea under consideration long before an outside inventor brings it to their attention. Some companies simply do not want to go through the torment that may be involved in negotiating with an outside inventor to use an idea. Some companies have found that inventors tend to grossly overrate the worth of their inventions, and reaching a suitable and reasonable agreement with these people is difficult, if not impossible.

Patents tend to be most useful and important to those about to manufacture a product embodying a patentable invention. When one is about to enter into the manufacture of a patentable product, many reasons support pursuing patent protection. One reason is that if patent protection is not pursued on the patentable features of the product, a competitor who independently makes the same invention may successfully pursue patent protection. Should this occur, one may be precluded from using his invention despite the fact that he may have been the first to invent. Another reason for urging that patent protection be pursued is to assure that competitors will not copy the unique and inventive features of a new product.

Still another important reason for patenting is to build a portfolio of patents covering one's products. Should the time arise when a manufacturer is faced with a charge of infringing a competitor's patent, it may be possible to dispose of the infringement charge by cross-licensing one of the manufacturer's patents in trade for a royalty-free license to use the competitor's patent. In short, patents can serve significant defensive, as well as offensive, functions for a manufacturer.

3-7   The Value of a Patent.   That large sums of money have been spent in obtaining a patent and all the machinery of the Patent and Trademark Office combined with the skills of the best patent attorneys have been used in an effort to insure patent validity do not mean the patent one obtains is inherently valuable. A patent merely gives evidence of one's right, for a limited period of time, to exclude others from using inventive property that may be worth much, little, or nothing.

Many of the patents granted each year are, from a commercial point of view, genuinely worthless. Some ingenious and meritorious inventions cannot, for one reason or another, be pursued commercially at a profit. Other inventions possessing little claim to either novelty or ingenuity may, through favorable conditions, prove to be sources of great wealth.

The monetary value of a patent does not depend so much on the intrinsic merit of the invention as on a multitude of external conditions affecting the chances, at a given point in time, of turning a particular invention into a profitable endeavor. The timeliness of an invention can decisively affect its commercial value. If the invention meets a recognized and keenly felt need, is workable, and is properly protected by a patent of good scope, one may predict with reasonable confidence that the patent has value.

When there is a pressing need accompanied by an already large demand, even a small but genuine improvement can become the basis of a very valuable patent. This may be the situation even though the improvement extends to little more than a slight savings in some established manufacture or technical process, the achievement of only a slightly superior product, or the mere acceleration of a production rate. There are many instances of fortunes being made from patents where the improvement was genuine, but very minor in character.

3-8 Benefits of a Patent System. Much has been written on the subject of why a viable patent system is essential to the technological development of a country. The patent system used in the United States evolved from the English common law, as first codified in 1623 by the British Statute of Monopolies. While a great many abuses of the British patent system had taken place by the time the founders of our country met at the Constitutional Convention in Philadelphia in 1787, the importance of encouraging the production and development of creative works was recognized by the incorporation of this provision into our Constitution at Article I, Section 8:

> The Congress shall have power . . . to promote the progress of science and useful arts, by securing for limited times to authors and inventors the exclusive right to their respective writings and discoveries.

Patents promote the progress of science and the useful arts by encouraging the disclosures of inventions tha would undoubtedly otherwise be kept secret. Patents assist the developers of new technology in protecting their investments so that they need not fear immediate competition from anyone who might otherwise seek to reap the benefits of one's costly research and development program. Patents stimulate competition by spurring competitors into maintaining a continuing program of inventive activity in efforts to obtain business advantage.

CHAPTER FOUR

What Can Be Patented and by Whom

For an invention to be patentable, it must meet several requirements set up to assure that patents are not issued irresponsibly. Some of these standards are complex to understand and apply. This chapter simplifies and summarizes the essence of these requirements.

4-1 Ideas, Inventions, and Patentable Inventions. "Invention" is a misleading term because it is used in so many different senses. In one, it refers to the act of inventing. In another, it refers to the product of the act of inventing. In still another, the term designates a patentable invention, the implication mistakenly being that if an invention is not patentable it is not an invention.

In the context of modern patent law, *invention* is the conception of a novel and useful contribution followed by its reduction to practice. *Conception* is the beginning of an invention; it is the creation in the mind of an inventor of a useful means for solving a particular problem. *Reduction to practice* can be either *actual*, as when an embodiment of the invention is tested to prove its successful operation under typical conditions of service, or *constructive*, as when a patent application is filed containing a complete description of the invention.

Ideas, per se, are not inventions and are not patentable. They are the tools of inventors, used in the development of inventions. Inventions are patentable only insofar as they meet certain criteria established by law. For an invention to be patentable, it must satisfy these conditions:

1. Fit within one of the statutorily recognized classes of patentable subject matter

2. Be the true and original product of the person seeking to patent the invention as its inventor

3. Be new at the time of its invention by the person seeking to patent it

4. Be useful in the sense of having some beneficial use in society

5. Be nonobvious to one of ordinary skill in the art to which the subject matter of the invention pertains at the time of its invention, and

6. Satisfy certain statutory bars that require the inventor to proceed with due diligence in pursuing efforts to file and prosecute a patent application.

4-2   The Requirement of Statutory Subject Matter.   As stated in the Supreme Court decision of *Kewanee Oil v. Bicron Corp.*, 416 U.S. 470, 181 USPQ 673 (1974), no patent is available for any discovery, however useful, novel, and nonobvious, unless it falls within one of the categories of patentable subject matter prescribed by Section 101 of Title 35 of the United States Code. Section 101 makes this provision:

> Whoever invents or discovers a new and useful process, machine, manufacture, or composition of matter, or any new and useful improvement thereof may obtain a patent therefor, subject to the conditions and requirements of this title.

The effect of establishing a series of statutory classes of eligible subject matter has been to limit the pursuit of patent protection to the useful arts. Patents directed to processes, machines, articles of manufacture, and compositions of matter have come to be referred to as utility patents inasmuch as these statutorily recognized classes encompass the useful arts.

Three of the four statutorily recognized classes of eligible subject matter may be thought of as products, namely, machines, manufactures, and compositions of matter. "Machine" has been interpreted in a relatively broad manner to include a wide variety of mechanisms and mechanical elements. "Manufactures" is essentially a catch-all term covering products other than machines and compositions of matter. "Compositions of matter," another broad term, embraces such elements as new molecules, chemical compounds, mixtures, alloys, and the like. "Manufactures" and "compositions of matter" arguably include such genetically engineered life forms that are not products of nature. The fourth class, "processes," relates to procedures leading to useful results.

Subject matter held to be ineligible for patent protection includes printed matter, products of nature, ideas, and scientific principles. Alleged inventions of perpetual motion machines are refused patents. A mixture of ingredients such as foods and medicines cannot be patented unless there is more to the mixture than the mere cumulative effect of its components. So-called patent medicines are seldom patented.

While no patent can be issued on an old product despite the fact that it has been found to be derivable through a new process, the new process for producing the product may well be patentable. That a product has been reduced to a purer state than was previously available in the prior art does not render the product patentable, but the process of purification may be patentable. A new use for an old product does not entitle one to obtain *product* patent protection, but may entitle one to obtain *process* patent protection, assuming the process meets other statutory requirements.

A newly discovered law of nature, regardless of its importance, is not entitled to patent protection. Methods of conducting business, and processes that either require a mental step to be performed or depend on aesthetic or emotional reactions have been held to not constitute statutory subject matter.

The patentability of computer-related inventions such as software and programmed machinery has been the subject of much debate in recent years. This topic has taken on sufficient importance to be treated separately in Chapter 21.

While the requirement of statutory subject matter falls principally within the bounds of 35 U.S.C. 101, other laws also operate to restrict the patenting of certain types of subject matter. For example, several statutes have been passed by Congress affecting patent rights in subject matter relating to atomic energy, aeronautics, and space. Still another statute empowers the Commissioner of Patents and Trademarks to issue secrecy orders regarding patent applications disclosing inventions that might be detrimental to the national security of the United States.

The foreign filing of patent applications on inventions made in the United States is prohibited for a brief period of time until a license has been granted by the Commissioner of Patents and Trademarks to permit foreign filing. This prohibition period enables the Patent and Trademark Office to review newly filed applications, locate any containing subject matter that may pose concerns to national security, and, after consulting with other appropriate agencies of government, issue secrecy orders preventing the contents of these applications from being disclosed publicly. If a secrecy order is issued, an inventor may be barred from filing applications abroad on penalty of imprisonment for up to 2 years, a $10,000 fine, or both. In the event a patent application is withheld under a secrecy order, the patent owner has a right to recover compensation from the government for damage caused by the secrecy order and/or for the use the government may have made of the invention.

Until only recently it was necessary for an inventor to wait six months (measured from the date of filing of an application) before proceeding with foreign filing, unless a license permitting expedited foreign filing was specifically requested from and granted by the Patent and Trademark Office. Now, however, licenses permitting expedited foreign filing are almost always granted automatically by the Office at the time of issuing an official filing receipt which advises the inventor of the filing date and serial number assigned to the application. Official filing receipts are now routinely being issued within a month of the date of filing, and bear a statement attesting to the grant of a foreign filing license.

4-3   The Requirement of Originality of Inventorship.   Under United States patent law, only the true and original inventor or inventors may apply to obtain patent protection. If the inventor has derived an invention from any other source or person, he is not entitled to apply for or obtain a patent.

The laws of our country are strict regarding the naming of the proper inventor or joint inventors in a patent application. When one person acting alone conceives an invention, he is the sole inventor and he alone must be named as the inventor in a patent application filed on that invention. When a plurality of people contribute to the conception of an invention, these persons must be named as joint inventors if they have contributed to the inventive features that are claimed in a patent application filed on the invention.

The concept of joint inventorship is recognized by statute, but is undefined. Joint inventorship is generally deemed to have occurred if two or more persons have collaborated in some fashion, with each contributing to conception. It is not necessary that exactly the same idea should have occurred to each of the collaborators at the same time.

When a substantial number of patentable features relating to a single overall development have occurred as the result of different combinations of sole inventors acting independently and/or joint inventors collaborating at different times, the patent law places a burden on the inventors to sort out "who invented what." Patent protection on the overall development must be pursued in the form of a number of separate patent applications, each directed to those patentable aspects of the development originating with a different inventor or group of inventors. In this respect, United States patent practice is unlike that of many foreign countries where the company for whom all the inventors work is often permitted to file a single patent application in its own name covering the overall development.

Misjoinder of inventors occurs when a person who is not a joint inventor has been named as such in a patent application. Nonjoinder of inventors occurs when there has been a failure to include a person who should have been named as a joint inventor. Misdesignation of inventorship occurs when none of the true inventors are named in an application. Only in recent years has correction of a misdesignation been permitted. If a problem of misjoinder, nonjoinder, or misdesignation has arisen without deceptive intent, provisions of the patent law permit correction of the error as long as such is pursued with diligence following the discovery.

4-4 The Requirement of Novelty.   Section 101 of Title 35 of the United States Code requires that a patentable invention be new. What is meant by "new" is defined in Sections 102(a), 102(e), and 102(g). Section 102(a) bars the issuance of a patent on an invention "known or used by others in this country, or patented or described in a printed publication in this or a foreign country, before the invention thereof by the applicant for patent." Section 102(e) bars the issuance of a patent on an invention "described in a patent granted on an application for patent by another filed in the United States before the invention thereof by the applicant for patent." Section 102(g) bars the issuance of a patent on an invention that "before the applicant's invention thereof . . . was made in this country by another who had not abandoned, suppressed, or concealed it."

These novelty requirements amount to negative rules of invention, the effect of which is to prohibit the issuance of a patent on an invention if the invention is not new. The novelty requirements of 35 U.S.C. 102 should not be confused with the statutory bar requirements of 35 U.S.C. 102, which are discussed in the last section of this chapter. A comparison of the novelty and statutory bar requirements of 35 U.S.C. 102 is presented in Table 2. The statutory bar requirements are distinguishable from the novelty requirements in that they do not relate to the newness of the invention, but to ways an inventor, who would otherwise have been able to apply for patent protection, has lost that right by tardiness.

To understand the novelty requirement of 35 U.S.C. 102, one must understand the concept of anticipation. A claimed invention is anticipated if a single prior art reference contains all the essential elements of the claimed invention. If teachings from more than one ref-

Table 2 Summary of the Novelty and Statutory Bar Requirements of 35 U.S.C. 102

Novelty Requirements

One may not patent an invention if, prior to its date of invention, the invention was any of the following:

1. Known or used by others in this country
2. Patented or described in a printed publication in this or a foreign country
3. Described in a patent granted on an application for patent by another filed in the United States
4. Made in this country by another who had not abandoned, suppressed, or concealed it.

Statutory Bar Requirements

One may not patent an invention he has previously abandoned. One may not patent an invention if, more than one year prior to the time his patent application is filed, the invention was any of the following:

1. Patented or described in a printed publication in this or a foreign country
2. In public use or on sale in this country
3. Made the subject of an inventor's certificate in a foreign country
4. Made the subject of a foreign patent application, which resulted in the issuance of a foreign patent before an application is filed in this country.

erence must be combined to show that the claimed combination of elements exists, there is no anticipation, and novelty exists. Combining references to render a claimed invention unpatentable brings into play the nonobviousness requirements of 35 U.S.C. 103, not the novelty requirement of 35 U.S.C. 102. Novelty hinges on anticipation and is a much easier concept to understand and apply than that of nonobviousness.

35 U.S.C. 102(a) Known or Used by Others in This Country Prior to the Applicant's Invention. In interpreting whether an invention has been known or used in this country, it has been held that the knowledge must consist of a complete and adequate description of the claimed invention and that this knowledge must be available, in some form, to the public. Prior use of an invention in this country by another will only be disabling if the invention in question has actually been reduced to practice and its use has been accessible to the public in some minimal sense. For a prior use to be disabling under Section 102(a), the use must have been of a complete and operable product or process that has been reduced to practice.

35 U.S.C. 102(a) Described in a Printed Publication in This or a Foreign Country Prior to the Applicant's Invention. For a printed publication to constitute a full anticipation of a claimed invention, the printed publication must adequately describe the claimed invention. The description must be such that it enables a person of ordinary skill in the art to which the invention pertains to understand and make the invention. The question of whether a *publication* has taken place is construed quite liberally by the courts to include almost any act that might legitimately constitute publication. The presence of a single thesis in a college library has been held to constitute publication. Similar liberality has been applied in construing the meaning of the term "printed."

35 U.S.C. 102(a) Patented in This or a Foreign Country. An invention is not deemed to be novel if it was patented in this country or any foreign country prior to the applicant's date of invention. For a patent to constitute a full anticipation and thereby render an invention unpatentable for lack of novelty, the patent must provide an adequate, operable description of the invention. The standard to be applied under Section 102(a) is whether the patent "describes" a claimed invention. A pending patent application is treated as constituting a "patent" for purposes of applying Section 102(a) as of the date of its issuance.

35 U.S.C. 102(e) Described in a Patent Filed in This Country Prior to the Applicant's Invention. Section 102(e) prescribes that if another inventor has applied to protect an invention before you invent the same invention, you cannot patent the invention. The effective date of a United States patent, for purposes of a Section 102(e) determination, is the filing date of its application rather than the date of patent issuance.

35 U.S.C. 102(g) Abandoned, Suppressed, or Concealed. For the prior invention of another person to stand as an obstacle to the novelty of one's invention under Section 102(g), the invention made by another must not have been abandoned, suppressed, or concealed. Abandonment, suppression, or concealment may be found when an inventor has been inactive for a significant period of time in pursuing reduction to practice of an invention. This is particularly true when the inventor's becoming active again has been spurred by knowledge of entry into the field of a second inventor.

4-5   The Requirement of Utility. To comply with the utility requirement of United States patent law, an invention must be capable of achieving some minimal useful purpose that is not illegal, immoral, or contrary to public policy. The invention must be operable and capable of being used for some beneficial purpose. The invention does not need to be a commercially successful product in order to satisfy the requirement of utility. While the requirement of utility is ordinarily a fairly easy one to meet, problems do occasionally arise with chemical compounds and processes, particularly in conjunction with various types of drugs. An invention incapable of being used to effect the proposed object of the invention may be held to fail the utility requirement.

4-6   The Requirement of Nonobviousness. The purpose of the novelty requirements of 35 U.S.C. 102 and the nonobvious requirement of 35 U.S.C. 103 are the same—to limit the issuance of patents to those innovations that do, in fact, advance the state of useful arts. While the requirements of novelty and nonobviousness may seem very much alike, the requirement of nonobviousness is a more sweeping one. This requirement maintains that if it would have been obvious (at the time an invention was made) to anyone ordinarily skilled in the art to produce the invention in the manner disclosed, then the invention does not rise to the dignity of a patentable invention and is therefore not entitled to patent protection.

The question of nonobviousness must be wrestled with by patent applicants in the event the Patent and Trademark Office rejects some or all their claims based on an assertion that the claimed invention is obvious in view of the teaching of one or a combination of two or more prior art references. When a combination of references is relied on in rejecting a claim, the argument the examiner is making is that it is obvious to combine the teachings of these references to produce the claimed invention. When such a rejection has been made, the burden is on the applicant to establish to the satisfaction of the examiner that the proposed combination of references would not have been obvious to one skilled in the art at the time the invention was made; and/ or that, even if the proposed combination of references is appropriate, it still does not teach or suggest the claimed invention.

In an effort to ascertain whether a new development is nonobvious, the particular facts and circumstances surrounding the development must be considered and weighed as a whole. Moreover, the question of nonobviousness must be judged as of the time the invention was made and in light of the then-existing knowledge and state of the art.

The test of nonobviousness has been found to be an extremely difficult one for courts to apply. The statutory language prescribing the nonobviousness requirement appears at Title 35, Section 103. It states:

> A patent may not be obtained . . . if the differences between the subject matter sought to be patented and the prior art are such that the subject matter as a whole would have been obvious at the time the invention was made to a person having ordinary skill in the art to which said subject matter pertains.

In the landmark decision of *Graham v. John Deere*, 383 U.S. 1, 148 USPQ 459 (1966), the United States Supreme Court held that several basic factual inquiries should be made in determining nonobviousness. These inquiries prescribe a four-step procedure or approach for judging nonobviousness. First, the scope and content of the prior art in the relevant field or fields must be ascertained. Second, the level of ordinary skill in the pertinent art is determined. Third, the differences between the prior art and the claims at issue are examined. Finally, a determination is made as to whether these differences would have been obvious to one of ordinary skill in the applicable art at the time the invention was made. Since the *Graham* ruling in 1966, a great deal of conflicting verbiage has appeared in court decisions interpreting what was intended by the *Graham* decision and confounding the meaning of nonobviousness. However, the rulings that are now being issued from the newly established United States Court of Appeals for the Federal Circuit (CAFC), which now hears (among other types of cases) all appeals in patent cases from the various federal district courts, are doing much to fulfill the long-felt need for a crisp, clean, and clear understanding of the proper test for nonobviousness. The CAFC is intellectually the finest court in many years to hear patent cases. It has made it clear that evidence of what are referred to as "secondary considerations" should be considered as part of all of the evidence in determining nonobviousness, not just when the decision maker remains in doubt after applying the four-step test of *Graham*. Secondary considerations include such things as commercial success of the invention in the marketplace, long-felt but unsatisfied need that is met by the invention, and prior failure by others who were trying to produce the same invention.

This brings us to the nonsubject of "synergism." In recent years, substantial consternation has arisen as the result of the supposed creation of a synergism test for nonobviousness. This test was said to have arisen from two Supreme Court decisions, one titled *Anderson's-Black Rock, Inc., v. Pavement Salvage Co., Inc.*, 396 U.S. 57, 163 USPQ 673 (1969), and the other titled *Sakraida v. Ag Pro, Inc.*,

425 U.S. 273, 189 USPQ 449 (1976). The concept of synergism has been said, by those mystics who have claimed to understand it, to arise when the combined effect of the several elements in a "combination patent"—a very poor term intended to refer to a patent that claims a combination-of-elements invention—amounts to more than the simple sum of the effects of the elements. The Court of Appeals of the Federal Circuit now has made it absolutely clear that such terms as "synergism" and "combination patent" are inappropriate, and that there is no support whatsoever for a synergism test in the patent statutes.

4-7   Statutory Bar Requirements.   Despite the fact that an invention may be new, useful, and nonobvious and that it may satisfy the other requirements of the patent law, an inventor can still lose the right to pursue patent protection on the invention unless he complies with certain requirements of the law called *statutory bars*. The statutory bar requirements assure that inventors will act with diligence in pursuing patent protection.

Since 35 U.S.C. 102 includes both the novelty and the statutory bar requirements of the law, the reader may wonder why the discussions of these two categories of requirements are not combined. Several reasons explain why these requirements should be considered separately. Section 102 is so easily misinterpreted that its content needs to be divided to be understood. Section 102 intertwines in a complex way the presentation of novelty and statutory bar requirements. The novelty requirements are basic to patentability in the same sense as are the requirements of statutory subject matter, originality, and nonobviousness. The statutory bar requirements are not basic to a determination of patentability, but rather operate to decline patent protection to an invention that may have been patentable at one time.

Section 102(b) bars the issuance of a patent if an invention was "in public use or on sale" in the United States more than one year prior to the date of the application for a patent. Section 102(c) bars the issuance of a patent if a patent applicant has previously abandoned the invention. Section 102(d) bars the issuance of a patent if the applicant has caused the invention to be first patented in a foreign country and has failed to file an application in the United States within one year after filing for a patent in a foreign country. Table 2 summarizes the statutory bar requirements of Section 102.

Once an invention has been made, the inventor is under no specific duty to file a patent application within any certain period of time. However, should one of the "triggering" events described in Section 102 occur, regardless of whether this occurrence may have been the result of action taken by the inventor or by actions of others, the inventor must apply for a patent within the prescribed period of time or be barred from obtaining a patent.

Some of the events that trigger statutory bar provisions are the patenting of an invention in this or a foreign country; the describing in a printed publication of the invention in this or a foreign country; public use of the invention in this country; or putting the invention on sale in this country. Some public uses and putting an invention on sale in this country will not trigger statutory bars if these activities were incidental to experimentation. Whether a particular activity amounts to experimental use has been the subject of much judicial dissension. The doctrine of experimental use is a difficult one to apply because of the conflicting decisions issued on this subject.

Certainly, the safest approach to take is to file for patent protection well within one year of the possibility of any statutory bar coming into play. If foreign patent protections are to be sought, the safest approach is to file an application in this country before any public disclosure is made of the invention. How one meets the "absolute novelty" requirements of certain foreign countries is discussed in Chapter 12.

CHAPTER FIVE

Preparing to Apply
for a Patent

Conducting a patentability search and preparing a patent application are two of the most important stages in efforts to pursue patent protection. This chapter points out pitfalls to avoid in both stages.

5-1 The Patentability Search. Conducting a patentability search prior to the preparation of a patent application can be extremely beneficial even when an inventor is convinced that no one has introduced a similar invention into the marketplace. A properly performed patentability study will guide not only the determination of the scope of patent protection to be sought, but also the claim-drafting approaches to be used. In almost every instance, a patent attorney who has at hand the results of a carefully conducted patentability study can do a better job of drafting a patent application, thereby helping to assure that it will be prosecuted smoothly, at minimal expense, through the rigors of examination in the Patent and Trademark Office.

Occasionally a patentability search will indicate that an invention is totally unpatentable. When this is the case, the search will have saved the inventor the cost of preparing and filing a patent application. At times a patentability search turns up one or more newly issued patents that pose infringement concerns. A patentability search is not, however, as extensive a search as is one conducted to locate possible infringement concerns when a great deal of money is being invested in a new product.

Some reasonable limitation is ordinarily imposed on the scope of a patentability search to keep search costs within a relatively small budget. The usual patentability search covers only United States patents and does not extend to foreign patents or to publications. Only the most pertinent Patent and Trademark Office subclasses are covered. However, despite the fact that patentability studies are not of exhaustive scope, a carefully conducted patentability search ordinarily can be relied on to give a decent indication of whether an invention is worthy of pursuing patent coverage to protect.

Searches do occasionally fail to turn up one or more pertinent references despite the best efforts of a competent searcher. Several reasons explain why a reference may be missed. One is that the files of the Public Search Room of the Patent and Trademark Office are incomplete. The Office estimates that as many as 7% of the Search Room references are missing or misfiled. Another reason is that the Public Search Room files do not contain some Patent Office subclasses. The searcher must review these missing subclasses in the "examiners' art," the files of patents used by examiners, where the examiners are free to remove references and take them to their offices as they see fit. Since most patents are cross-referenced in several subclasses, a careful searcher will try to assure that the search is carried out in a sufficient number of pertinent subclasses so that if a pertinent patent was missed in searching one subclass, it will be found elsewhere.

5-2   Putting the Invention in Proper Perspective.   It is vitally important that a client takes whatever time is needed to make certain that his patent attorney fully understands the character of the invention before the attorney undertakes the preparation of a patent application. The patent attorney should be given an opportunity to talk with those involved in the development effort from which an invention has emerged. He should be told what features these people believe are important to protect. Moreover, the basic history of the art to which the invention relates should be described, together with a discussion of the efforts made by others to address the problems solved by the present invention.

The client should also convey to his patent attorney how the present invention fits into the client's overall scheme of developmental activities. Much can be done in drafting a patent application to lay the groundwork for protection of future developments. Additionally, one's patent attorney needs to know how product liability concerns may arise with regard to the present invention, so that the statements he makes in the patent application will not be used to client's detriment in product liability litigation. Personal injury lawyers have been known to scrutinize the representations a manufacturer makes in his patents to find language that will assist in obtaining recoveries for persons injured by patented as well as nonpatented inventions.

Before preparation of an application is begun, careful consideration should be given to the scope and type of claims that will be included. In many instances, it is possible to pursue both process and product claims. Also, in many instances, it is possible to present claims approaching the invention from varying viewpoints so different combinations of features can be covered. Frequently, it is possible to couch at least two of the broadest claims in different language so efforts of competitors to design around the claim language will be frustrated.

Careful consideration must be given to approaches that competitors may take in efforts to design around the claimed invention. The full range of invention equivalents must be determined to the best of the abilities of the inventor and his attorney so claims of appropriate scope will be presented in the resulting application.

5-3   Preparing the Application.   A properly prepared patent application is a work of art. It should be a readable and understandable teaching document. If it is not, insist that your patent attorney rework the document. A patent application that accurately describes an invention without setting forth the requisite information in a clear and convincing format may be legally sufficient, but it does not represent the quality of work a client has the right to expect.

A well-drafted patent application should explain accurately, yet interestingly, the background of the invention and the character of the problems that are overcome. It should discuss the closest prior art known to the applicant and should indicate how the invention patentably differs from prior art proposals. It should present a summary of the invention that brings out the major advantages of the invention and explains how prior art drawbacks are overcome. These elements of a patent application may occupy several typed pages. They constitute an introduction to the remainder of the document.

Following this introductory section, the application should present a brief description of such drawings as may accompany the application. Then follows a detailed description of the best mode known to the inventor for carrying out the invention. In the detailed description, one or more preferred embodiments of the invention are described in sufficient detail to enable a person having ordinary skill in the art to which the invention relates to practice the invention. While some engineering details such as dimensions, materials of construction, circuit component values, and the like may be omitted, all details critical to the practice of the invention must be included. If there is any question about the essential character of a detail, prudent practice would dictate its inclusion.

The written portion of the application concludes with a series of claims. The claims are the most difficult part of the application to prepare. Even though the claims tend to be the most confusing part of the application, the applicant should spend enough time wrestling with the claims and/or the patent attorney to make certain the content of the claims is fully understood. Legal gibberish should be avoided, such as endless uses of the word "said." Elements unessential to the practice of the invention should be omitted from the claims. Essential elements should be described in the broadest possible terms in at least some of the claims so the equivalents of the preferred embodiment of the invention will be covered.

The patent application will usually include one or more sheets of drawings and will be accompanied by a suitable declaration or oath to be signed by the inventor or inventors. The drawings of a patent application should illustrate each feature essential to the practice of the invention, and should show every feature to which reference is made in the claims. The drawings must comply in size and format with several very technical rules promulgated by the Patent and Trademark Office. The preparation of patent drawings is ordinarily best left to an experienced patent draftsperson.

If a patent application is prepared properly, it should pave the way for smooth handling of the patent application during its prosecution. If a patent application properly tells the story of the invention, it should constitute a teaching document that will stand on its own and be capable of educating a court regarding the character of the art to which the invention pertains, as well as the import of this invention to that art. Since patent suits are tried before judges who rarely have technical backgrounds, it is important that a patent application make an effort to present the basic features of the invention in terms understandable by those having no technical training. It is unusual for an invention to be so impossibly complex that its basic thrust defies description in fairly simple terms. A patent application is suspect if it wholly fails to, at some point, set forth the pith of the invention in terms a grade-school student can grasp.

5-4 Enablement, Best Mode, Description, and Distinctness Requirements. Once a patent application has been prepared and is in the hands of the inventor for review, it is important that the inventor keep in mind the enablement, best mode, description, and distinctness requirements of the patent law.

The enablement requirement calls for the patent application to present sufficient information to enable a person skilled in the relevant art to make and use the invention. The disclosure presented in the application must be such that it does not require one skilled in the art to experiment to any appreciable degree to practice the invention.

The best mode requirement mandates that an inventor disclose, at the time he files a patent application, the best mode he then knows about for carrying out or practicing the invention.

The description requirement also relates to the descriptive part of a patent application and the support it must provide for any claims that may need to be added after the application has been filed. Even though a patent application may adequately teach how to make and use the subject matter of the claimed invention, a problem can arise during the prosecution of a patent application where one determines it is desirable to add claims differing in language from those filed originally. If the claim language one wants to add does not find full support in the originally filed application, the benefit of the original filing date will be lost with regard to the subject matter of the claims to be added. Therefore, in reviewing a patent application prior to its being executed, an inventor should keep in mind that the description that forms a part of the application should include support for any language he may later want to incorporate in the claims of the application.

The distinctness requirement applies to the content of the claims. In reviewing the claims of a patent application, an inventor should endeavor to make certain that the claims particularly point out and distinctly claim the subject matter that he regards as his invention. The claims must be definite in the sense that their language must clearly set forth the area over which an applicant seeks exclusive rights. The language used in the claims must find support in the earlier descriptive portion of the application. The claims must not include within their scope of coverage any prior art known to the inventor, and yet should present the invention in the broadest possible terms that patentably distinguish the invention over the prior art.

5-5 Functional Language in Claims. While functional language in claims may tend to draw objection, there is statutory support for using a particular type of functional claim language. Section 112 of Title 35 of the United States Code includes this statement:

> An element in a claim for a combination may be expressed as a *means* or step *for performing* a specified *function* without the recital of structure, material, or acts in support thereof, and such claim shall be construed to cover the corresponding structure, material, or acts described in the specification and equivalents thereof. (Emphasis Added)

Using a "means plus function" format to claim an invention can be one of the most effective approaches to take in an effort to achieve the broadest possible coverage of alternative approaches that competitors may explore. However, in drafting a claim in means-plus-function format, care must be taken to assure that what is being claimed amounts to more than a *single means* (i.e., a single element defined in means-plus-function format), for the requirement of the patent law that means-plus-function language be used only in a claim for a combination is not met by such a claim. Such a claim is deemed to be of undue breadth for, in essence, it claims every conceivable means for achieving a stated result.

5-6 Product-by-Process Claims. In some instances it is possible to claim a product by describing the process or method of its manufacture. Traditionally, the Patent and Trademark Office has taken the position that product-by-process claims are permissible only when the product cannot be defined adquately in any other fashion. Since 1974, however, product-by-process claims have been deemed allowable by the Patent and Trademark Office even if the product can be described in purely structural terms, so long as other claim requirements, such as definiteness, are properly met. Some examiners still adhere to the more traditional view of the impropriety of product-by-process claims, and difficulties continue to be encounterd in obtaining the allowance of these types of claims universally throughout the Patent and Trademark Office.

5-7 Claim Format. Each claim is a complete sentence. In many instances the first part of the sentence of each claim appears at the beginning of the claims section and reads "What is claimed is:" Each claim typically includes three parts: a preamble, a transition, and a body. The *preamble* is the part that introduces the claim by summarizing the field of the invention, its relation to the prior art, and its intended use, or the like. The *transition* is a word or phrase connecting the preamble to the body. The terms "comprises" or "comprising" often perform this function. The *body* is the listing of elements and limitations that define the scope of what is being claimed.

Claims are either *independent* or *dependent*. An independent claim stands on its own and makes no reference to any other claim. A dependent claim refers to another claim which may be independent or dependent, and adds to the subject matter of the referenced claim. If a dependent claim depends from (makes reference to) more than one other claim, it is called a *multiple dependent claim*.

One type of claim format that can be used gained notoriety in a 1917 decision of the Commissioner of Patents in a case styled *Ex parte Jepson*, 1917 C.D. 62. In a claim of the Jepson format, the preamble recites all the elements deemed to be old, the body of the claim includes only such new elements as constitute improvements, and the transition separates the old from the new. The Patent and Trademark Office favors the use of Jepson-type claims since this type of claim is thought to assist in segregating what is old in the art from what the applicant claims as his invention.

In 1966, the Patent and Trademark Office sought to encourage the use of Jepson-type claims by prescribing the following Rule 75(e):

> Where the nature of the case admits, as in the case of an improvement, any independent claim should contain in the following order, (1) a preamble comprising a general description of the elements or steps of the claimed combination which are conventional or known, (2) a phrase such as "wherein the improvement comprises," and (3) those elements, steps and/or relationships which constitute that portion of the claimed combination which the applicant considers as the new or improved portion.

Thankfully, the use of the term "should" in Rule 75(e) makes use of Jepson-type claims permissive rather than mandatory. Many instances occur when it is desirable to include several distinctly old elements in the body of a claim. The preamble in a Jepson-type claim has been held to constitute a limitation for purposes of determining patentability and infringement, while the preambles of claims presented in other types of formats may not constitute limitations. A proper understanding of the consequences of presenting claims in various types of formats and the benefits thereby obtained will be taken into account by one's patent attorney.

5-8 Executing the Application. Once an inventor has satisfied himself with the content of a proposed patent application, he should read carefully the oath or declaration accompanying the application.

The required content of this formal document recently has been simplified. In it the inventor states that he:

1. Has reviewed and understands the content of the specification, including the claims, as amended by any amendment specifically referred to in the oath or declaration
2. Believes the named inventor or inventors to be the original and first inventor or inventors of the subject matter which is claimed and for which a patent is sought
3. Acknowledges the duty to disclose to the Patent and Trademark Office during examination of the application information which is material to the examination of the application.

If the application is being filed as a division, continuation, or continuation-in-part of one or more co-pending parent applications, the parent case or cases are identified in the oath or declaration. Additionally, if a claim to the benefit of a foreign-filed application is being made, it is recited in the oath or declaration.

Absolutely no changes should be made in any part of a patent application once it has been executed. If some change, no matter how ridiculously minor, is found to be required after an application has been signed, the executed oath or declaration must be destroyed and a new one signed after the application has been corrected. If an application is executed without having been inspected by the applicant or is altered after having been executed, it may be stricken from the files of the Patent and Trademark Office.

5-9 Patent and Trademark Office Fees.   The Office charges a fee to file an application, a fee to issue a patent, and a host of other fees for such things as obtaining an extension of time to respond to an Office Action.

Effective October 1, 1982, a very dramatic increase in almost all fees was implemented. The most striking result of these fee increases was the dramatic increase in applications filed during September 1982, as the date of the fee increase drew increasingly near. I, too, stood in the lengthy line that snaked through the lobby of Crystal Plaza Two in September to file the applications prepared for our clients during that month in order to take advantage of the then-applicable filing fees. The sight of half a dozen Office clerks stamping in applications and tossing them into crates as fast as the papers could be made airborne was an unprecedented picture I shall long remember.

As of this writing, the *basic fee* required to file a patent application has increased six-hundred-fold to $300 since it was first set at 50 cents under the patent act of 1790. From 1965 through October 1, 1982, the basic fee for filing a utility application stood at $65, with additional charges being made for claims in excess of a total of 10 and independent claims in excess of 1.

In addition to the basic fee of $300, $30 is charged for each independent claim in excess of a total of 3; $10 is charged for each claim of any kind in excess of a total of 20; and $100 is charged for any application that includes one or more multiple dependent claims. However, if the applicant is entitled to claim the benefits of *small entity status*, the entire filing fee is halved, as are most other fees that are associated with the handling of a patent application.

The filing fee for a design application presently stands at $125 unless small entity status is established, whereupon this fee also may be halved.

New rules now permit the Office to assign a filing date before the filing fee and oath or declaration have been received. While the filing fee and an oath or declaration are still needed to complete an application, a filing date will now be assigned as of the date of receipt of the specification and any required drawing.

The *issue fee* charged by the Office for issuing a utility patent on an allowed application stands at $500. Small entity status reduces this fee to $250. The issue fee for a design application is $175, which also may be halved with the establishment of small entity status.

Maintenance fees have been enacted to keep an issued utility patent in force during its term. No maintenance fees are charged on design or plant patents, or on utility patents that have issued from applications filed before December 12, 1980. Patents issuing on applications filed from December 12, 1980, through August 26, 1982, stand at $200, $400, and $600, to be paid, respectively, no later than $3\frac{1}{2}$ years, $7\frac{1}{2}$ years and $11\frac{1}{2}$ years from their dates of issuance, with no small entity status reductions being available. Patents issuing on applications filed after August 26, 1982, stand at $400, $800, and $1200 (with small entity "half-price" reductions being available), to be paid, respectively, no later than $3\frac{1}{2}$ years, $7\frac{1}{2}$ years, and $11\frac{1}{2}$ years from their issuance dates.

5-10 Small Entity Status. The practice of providing half-price fees to individual inventors, nonprofit organizations, and small businesses came into existence concurrently with the implementation of the fee increase of October 1, 1982.

Qualification for small entity status requires only the filing of a verified statement prior to or with the first fee paid as a small entity. Statements as to qualification as a small entity must be filed by all entities having rights with respect to an application or patent in order to qualify. Once qualification has been achieved, there is a continuing duty to advise the Office before paying the next fee if qualification for small entity status has been lost.

Those who qualify for small entity status include:

1. A sole inventor who has not transferred his rights and is under no obligation to transfer his rights to an entity that fails to qualify

2. Joint inventors where no one among them has transferred his rights and is under no obligation to transfer his rights to an entity that fails to qualify

3. A nonprofit organization such as an institution of higher education or an IRS qualified and exempted nonprofit organization

4. A small business which has not more than 500 employees after taking into account the average number of employees (including full time, part time, and temporary) during the fiscal year of the business entity in question and of its affiliates. The term

"affiliate" is defined by a broad-reaching "control" test which holds that concerns are "affiliates" of each other when either, directly or indirectly, "controls or has the power to control" the other, or when a third party or parties "controls or has the power to control" both concerns.

Any attempt to fraudulently establish small entity status, or establishing such status improperly and through gross negligence is considered a fraud on the Office. An application could be disallowed for such an act. Failure to establish small entity status on a timely basis forfeits the right to small entity status benefits with respect to a fee being paid unless small entity status is promptly established and a refund promptly requested. A good-faith error made in establishing small entity status may be excused by paying any deficient fees. However, if the payment is made more than three months after the error occurred, a verified statement establishing good faith and explaining the error must be filed.

5-11 Express Mail Filing. During 1983 a new procedure was adopted by the Office which permits any paper or fee to be filed with the Office by utilizing the Express Mail Post Office to Addressee service of the United States Postal Service. When this is done, the filing date of the paper or fee will be that shown on the Express Mail mailing label.

To qualify for the filed-when-mailed advantage, each paper must bear the number of the Express Mail mailing label, must be addressed to the Commissioner of Patents and Trademarks, Washington, D.C. 20231, and must include a certificate of mailing by Express Mail signed by the person who makes the actual mail deposit.

The practical and very important effect of this new procedure is to eliminate the hassle that has long been associated with the last-minute attempts to effect physical delivery of patent applications to the Office in time to meet a bar date or comply with a convention filing date.

CHAPTER SIX

Prosecuting a Pending
Patent Application

Once an executed patent application has been received by the Patent and Trademark Office, the patent application is said to be pending. The prosecution period of a patent application is the time during which an application is pending; it begins when a patent application is filed in the Patent and Trademark Office and continues until either a patent is granted or the application is abandoned. The activities that take place during this time are referred to as *prosecution*.

6-1 Patent Pending.   Once an application for a patent has been received by the Patent and Trademark Office, the applicant may mark products embodying the invention with an indication of "Patent Pending" or "Patent Applied For." These expressions mean a patent application has been filed and has neither been abandoned nor issued as a patent. The terms do not mean the Patent and Trademark Office has taken up examination of the merits of an application, much less approved the application for issuance as a patent.

The fact that a patent application has been filed, or is pending or applied for, does not provide any protection against infringement by competitors. While pending patent applications are held in secrecy by the Patent and Trademark Office and therefore do not constitute a source of information available to competitors regarding the activities of an inventor, nothing prevents competitors from independently developing substantially the same invention and seeking to market it. Neither is there any legal basis for stopping a competitor from purchasing a product bearing a designation "Patent Pending" and copying the invention embodied in the purchased product.

As a practical matter, however, marking products with the designation "Patent Pending" often has the effect of discouraging competitors from copying an invention, whereby the term of the patent that eventually issues may effectively be extended to include the period during which the application is pending. In many instances, competitors will not risk an substantial investment in preparation for the manufacture and merchandising of a product marked with the designation "Patent Pending," for they know their efforts may be legally interrupted as soon as a patent issues.

6-2   Secrecy of Pending Applications.   With the exception of applications filed to reissue existing patents, pending patent applications are maintained in strictest confidence by the Patent and Trademark Office. No information regarding a pending application will be given out by the Office without authority from the applicant or owner of the application. However, if an interested third party learns of the pendency of an application, he may file a protest to its issuance, as is discussed in Section 7-8.

The file of a pending application can only be inspected as a matter of right by the named inventor, an assignee of record, an exclusive licensee, an attorney of record, or such persons as have received written authority from someone permitted by right to inspect the file. This provision of secrecy extends to abandoned applications, as well as to pending applications. In the event an abandoned application is referred to in an issued patent, access to the file of the abandoned case will be granted to members of the public on request. Should a pending patent application be referred to in an issued patent, access may usually be obtained by petition. All reissue applications are open to inspection by the general public. The filing of a protest in a reissue application is discussed in Section 7-8.

6-3   Duty of Candor.   The Patent and Trademark Office has placed increased emphasis on the duty an applicant has to deal candidly with the Patent and Trademark Office.

In accordance with Patent Office guidelines, a patent applicant is urged to submit an Information Disclosure Statement either concurrently with the filing of an application or within three months of its filing. When these guidelines were implemented in 1977, what are now called Information Disclosure Statements were referred to as Prior Art Statements. An Information Disclosure Statement may be either separate from or incorporated in a patent application. It should include a listing of patents, publications, or other information that is believed to be "material," and a concise explanation of the relevance of each listed item. Items are deemed to be "material" where there is a "substantial likelihood that a reasonable examiner would consider it important in deciding whether to allow the application to issue as a patent."

The courts have held that those who participate in proceedings before the Office have the "highest duty of candor and good faith." While the courts differ markedly in their holding of the consequences of misconduct, fraud on the Patent and Trademark Office has been found to be a proper basis for taking a wide variety of punitive actions such as striking applications from the records of the Office, canceling issued patents, denying enforcement of patents in infringement actions, awarding attorney's fees to defendants in infringement actions, and imposing criminal sanctions on those who were involved in fraudulently procuring patents. Inequitable conduct other than outright fraud has been recognized as a defense against enforcement of a patent, as a basis for awarding attorney's fees in an infringement action, and as a basis of antitrust liability.

In short, the duty of candor one has in dealings with the Office should be taken very seriously. Prudent practice would urge that if there is any question concerning whether a reference or other facts are "material," a citation should be made promptly to the Office so that the examiner can decide the issue.

6-4   Initial Review of Application.   Promptly after an application is filed, it is examined to make certain it is complete and satisfies formal requirements sufficiently to permit its being assigned a filing date and serial number. Once a patent application has been received by the Patent and Trademark Office and assigned a filing date and serial number, the classification of the subject matter of the claimed invention is determined and the application is assigned to the appropriate examining group. In the group, the application is assigned to a particular examiner. Each examiner takes the applications assigned to him in the order of their filing.

The Patent and Trademark Office receives nearly 2000 patent applications per week. Although nearly 1400 examiners staff the Office, a backlog of several months of cases awaits action in most of the examining sections called Group Art Units. This results in a delay of several months between the time an application is filed and when it receives its first thorough examination on the merits.

Once an examiner reaches an application and begins the initial review, he checks the application still further for compliance with formal requirements and conducts a search of the prior art to determine the novelty and nonobviousness of the claimed invention. The examiner prepares an Office Action in which he notifies the applicant of any objections to the application, any requirements regarding election of certain claims for present prosecution, and/or any rejections he believes should be made of the claims.

In the event the examiner deems all the claims in the application to be patentable, he notifies the applicant of this fact and issues a Notice of Allowance. It troubles me to receive a Notice of Allowance on the first Office Action. While I do not file applications with claims that are broader than I think a client is entitled to receive, if a Notice of Allowance issues on the first Office Action, I am left with the nagging feeling that had I sought claims of even broader scope, perhaps they too might have been allowed.

In some instances, the examiner will find it necessary to object to the form of the application. Hopefully, these formal objections are not debilitating and can be corrected by relatively minor amendments made in response to the Office Action.

In treating the merits of the claims, especially in a first Office Action, it is not uncommon for an examiner to reject a majority, if not all, of the claims. Some examiners feel strongly that they have a duty to encourage the inventor to put on record his reasons for believing that the claimed invention is patentable. They achieve this objective by citing the closest art they are able to find and by presenting rejections based on this art. Doing this forces the inventor to respond by arguing for patentability of the invention.

6-5   Response to Office Action.   In the event the first Office Action issued by an examiner is adverse in any respect, the applicant may reply in almost any form that constitutes a bona fide attempt to advance the prosecution of the application. The applicant is entitled to at least one reexamination following the issuance of the first Office Action, even if the response filed by the applicant amounts to nothing more than a request for reconsideration.

Since the file of a patent application will become open to public inspection on the issuance of a patent, and because an issued patent must be interpreted in view of the content of its file, the character of any arguments presented to the Patent and Trademark Office in support of a claimed invention are critical. In responding to an Office Action it is essential that care be taken in the drafting of arguments to assure that no misrepresentations are made and that the arguments will not result in an unfavorable interpretation of allowed claims being made during the years when the resulting patent is in force.

It is important that every effort be made to advance the prosecution of the application in responding to an Office Action. While in previous years it was not unusual for half a dozen or more Office Actions to issue during the course of pendency of a patent application, in more recent years the Office has placed emphasis on compacting the prosecution of patent applications. Today it is not unusual for the prosecution of a patent application to be concluded on the issuance of the second or third Office Action. In an increasing number of cases, a final rejection is made as early as the second or third Office Action.

When an Office Action is mailed from the Patent and Trademark Office, a time period for filing a response begins. In the event a response is not filed within the time set by law, the application will automatically become abandoned, and rights to a patent may be lost forever. Ordinarily, a response must be filed within a three-month period from the mailing date of the Office Action. An extension of time of up to three months can be had so long as the statutory requirement of filing a response within six months of the issuance of an Office Action is met. In previous years, it was necessary to present reasons to justify the grant of an extension of time, and the grant of an extension request was discretionary. Now, however, extensions are granted automatically upon receipt of a petition for extension accompanied by a proper response to the Office Action and the required fee. The fee for obtaining an extension of time increases as the number of months covered by the extension increases.

Each objection and rejection made by the examiner must be treated when responding to an Office Action. If the inventor agrees that certain of his claims should not be allowed in view of art cited by the examiner, these claims may be cancelled or amended to better distinguish the invention over the cited art.

Typical responses to Office Actions involve the addition, cancellation, substitution, or amendment of claims; the amendment of the descriptive portion of the application can be done if no "new matter" is added by the amendment; and the presentation of arguments regarding the allowability of the claimed invention in which explanations are provided about how the claims patentably distinguish themselves over the cited references. A response may also include the submission of an affidavit to overcome a cited reference either by establishing a date of invention before the effective date of the reference or by presenting factual evidence supporting patentability over the reference.

If the Office has objected to the drawings, corrections must now be made either by utilizing the services of a bonded patent drafting service that has been approved by the Office, or by substituting drawings that include the required corrections.

6-6   Reexamination Following a Response.   Once the applicant has responded, the examiner reexamines the case and issues a second Office Action apprising the applicant of his findings. If the examiner agrees to allow all the claims that remain active in the application, prosecution on the merits is closed and the application may not present further amendments or add other claims as a matter of right. If the Office Action is adverse with regard to the merits of the claims, the prosecution of the case continues until such time as the examiner issues an Office Action including a final rejection.

The examiner makes a rejection *final* once a clear and unresolved issue has developed between the examiner and the applicant. After a final rejection has issued, the character of the responses that may be made by the applicant is limited. The applicant may appeal the final rejection to an intra-agency Board of Appeals, cancel the rejected claims, comply with all of the requirements for allowance if any have been laid down by the examiner, or file a continuation application whereby the examination procedure is begun again.

In the majority of instances during the period of prosecution, the application eventually reaches a form acceptable to the examiner handling the application, and the examiner will issue a Notice of Allowance. If it is impossible to reach accord with the examiner handling the application, the inventor can make use of the procedures for appeal.

If an initial appeal taken to the Board of Appeals should result in an unfavorable decision, a further appeal may be taken either to the United States District Court for the District of Columbia, or to the newly established United States Court of Appeals for the Federal Circuit (which, as of October 1, 1982, replaced what was previously known as the United States Court of Customs and Patent Appeals). In some instances, further appeals may be pursued to higher courts.

One recently adopted practice of the Office which concerns many attorneys is worthy of mention. When the record of an application "does not otherwise reveal the reasons for allowance," an examiner may put a comment in the file to explain his reasons for allowing a case. While fine in theory, this practice has tended to result in examiners making very simplistic statements that focus on a single reason. If the reason stated by an examiner for allowing a patent is shown during litigation to be faulty, this can cause the patent to be held invalid. Accordingly, if a communication is received from the Office stating a reason for allowance, it should be reviewed with care. Often it is desirable to exercise one's right to promptly comment on the stated reason, for despite a statement in Office Rule 109 to the contrary, failure to comment may in real-world practice give rise to an implication that the applicant agrees.

6-7 Interviewing the Examiner. If, during the prosecution of a patent application, it appears that substantial differences of opinion or possible misunderstandings are being encountered in dealing with the examiner to whom the application has been assigned, it is advisable for the attorney to conduct a personal interview with the examiner.

Considering the relatively sterile and terse nature of many Office Actions, it is often impossible to determine accurately what the examiner's opinion may be regarding how the application should be prosecuted further. While the word processing equipment acquired by the Office has made it easier for examiners to expound the reasons underlying their rejections, situations still arise where it is quite clear that an examiner and an attorney are not communicating in the full sense of the word. At times, a personal interview will be found to provide valuable guidance for bringing the prosecution of the application to a successful conclusion. In other instances, an interview will be beneficial in ascertaining the true character of any difference of opinion between the applicant and the examiner, thereby enabling the exact nature of this issue to be addressed thoroughly in the next response filed by the applicant.

6-8 Restriction and Election Requirements. If a patent examiner determines that an application contains claims to more than one independent and distinct invention, the examiner may impose what is called a *restriction requirement*. In the event the examiner finds that the application claims alternative modes or forms of an invention, he may require the applicant to elect one of these species for present prosecution. This is called a *species election requirement*. Once a restriction or election requirement has been imposed, the applicant must elect one of the designated inventions or species for present prosecution in the original application. The applicant may file divisional applications on the nonelected inventions or species any time during the pendency of the original application.

When responding to an Office Action that includes a restriction and/or election requirement, it is usually desirable to present arguments in an effort to traverse the requirement and request its reconsideration. After traversing, the examiner is obliged to reconsider the requirement, but he may repeat it and make it final. Sometimes the examiner can be persuaded to modify or withdraw a restriction and/or election requirement, thereby permitting a larger number of claims to be considered during the prosecution of the pending application. Where a restriction and/or election requirement has been traversed (opposed by requesting reconsideration for stated reasons), upon allowance of elected claims, the Office will notify the applicant that the application is in condition for allowance except for the presence of such claims as remain in the case and are directed to a nonelected invention or species. The applicant will then be given a month to take appropriate action such as the filing of a divisional application or the filing of a petition for reconsideration of an election requirement. As a practical matter, unless the examiner has set out a restriction and/or election requirement that is utterly and completely absurd, a petition seeking reconsideration is usually a waste of effort. Thankfully it is seldom that an examiner decides that a simple application defines two dozen separate inventions, whereby the need to petition is a rarity.

6-9   Double Patenting Rejections.   Occasionally, one may receive a rejection based on the doctrine of double patenting. This doctrine precludes the issuance of a second patent on the same invention already claimed in a previously issued patent.

One approach to overcoming a double patenting rejection is to establish a clear line of demarcation between the claimed subject matter of the second application and that of the earlier patent. If the line of demarcation is such that the claimed subject matter of the pending application is nonobvious in view of the invention claimed in the earlier patent, no double patenting rejection is proper. If the claimed subject matter of the pending application defines merely an obvious variation of the claimed invention of the earlier issued patent, the double patenting rejection may be overcome by the filing of a *terminal disclaimer*. The terminal portion of any patent issuing on the pending application is disclaimed so that any patent issuing on the pending application will expire on the same day the already-existing patent expires. If the claimed subject matter of the pending application is identical to the claimed subject matter in the earlier issued patent, it is not possible to establish a line of demarcation between the two cases, and the pending application is not patentable even if a terminal disclaimer is filed.

The courts have held that double patenting problems can occur when a utility patent application and a design patent application have been filed on the same invention. The fact that both a utility patent and a design patent may have issued on various features of a common invention does not necessarily mean a double patenting problem exists. If it is possible to practice the ornamental appearance covered by the design patent without necessarily infringing any of the claims of the utility patent, and if it is possible to practice the claimed invention of the utility patent without infringing the ornamental appearance covered by the design patent, no double patenting problem is present.

6-10 Patent Issuance. Once a Notice of Allowance has been mailed by the Office, the applicant has a period of three months to pay the issue fee. A patent will not issue unless this fee is paid. A few weeks before the patent issues, the Office mails a Notice of Issuance which advises the applicant of the issue date and patent number.

Once a patent issues, its file history is no longer held secret. The several documents that form the complete file history of a patent are referred to collectively as the *file wrapper*.

Upon receipt of a newly issued patent, it should be reviewed with care to check for printing errors. If printing errors of misleading or otherwise significant nature are detected, it is desirable to petition for a certificate of correction. If errors of a clerical or typographical nature have been made by the applicant or by the attorney, and if these errors are not the fault of the Patent and Trademark Office, a fee must be paid to obtain the issuance of a certificate of correction. If the errors are the fault of the Patent and Trademark Office, no such fee need be paid.

6-11   Safeguarding the Original Patent Document.   The original patent document merits appropriate safeguarding. It is printed on heavy bond paper, its pages are fastened together by a silk ribbon, and it is sealed by the Official Seal of the United States Patent and Trademark Office. The patent owner should preserve this original document in a safe place as evidence of his proprietary interest in the invention. If an infringer must be sued, the patent owner may be called on to produce his original patent in court.

6-12   Continuation, Division, and Continuation-in-Part Applications.   During the pendency of an application, it may be desirable to file either a continuation or a divisional application. A continuation application may be filed if the prosecution of a pending application has not proceeded as desired, whereby a further opportunity for reconsideration can be had before an appeal is taken. A divisional application may be filed when two or more inventions are disclosed in the original application, and claims to only one of these inventions are deemed to be proper for examination in the originally filed case. The divisional application picks up the claims that were not permitted to be examined in the parent application.

It frequently occurs during the pendency of a patent application that a continuing research and development program being conducted by the inventor results in improvements in the original invention. Because of a prohibition in the patent law against amending the content of a pending patent application to include "new matter," any improvements made in the invention after the time an application is filed cannot be incorporated into the pending application. When improvements are made that are deemed to merit patent protection, a continuation-in-part application is filed. Such an application can be filed only during the pendency of an earlier-filed application commonly called the *parent* case. The continuation-in-part case receives the benefit of the filing date of the parent application with regard to such subject matter as is common to the parent application. Any subject matter uncommon to the parent application is entitled only to the benefit of the filing date of the continuation-in-part case.

In some instances when a continuation-in-part application has been filed, the improvement that forms the new subject matter of the continuation-in-art case is closely associated with the subject matter of the earlier-filed application, and the earlier application can be abandoned in favor of the continuation-in-part case. In other instances, the new matter that forms the basis of the continuation-in-part application clearly constitutes an invention in and of itself. In such a situation it may be desirable to continue the prosecution of the original application to obtain one patent that covers the invention claimed in the original application, and a second patent that covers the improvement invention.

6-13   Maintaining a Chain of Pending Applications.   If a continuing development program is underway and produces a series of new improvements, it can be advantageous to maintain on file in the Patent and Trademark Office a continuing series of pending applications. If an original parent application is filed initially, and a series of continuation, division, and/or continuation-in-part applications are filed in such a manner that assures the existence of an uninterrupted chain of pending cases, any patent or patents that may issue on the earlier cases cannot be used as references against later applications in the chain. This technique of maintaining a series or chain of pending applications is an especially important technique to use when the danger exists that the closest prior art the Office may be able to cite against the products of continuing research and development effort is the patent protection that issued on early aspects of the overall effort.

CHAPTER SEVEN

Using an Issued Patent

This chapter points out several basics that need to be kept in mind to maximize the benefits obtained from an issued patent. The procedures involved in enforcing a patent against an infringer are discussed, and the character of an interference proceeding is described as well.

7-1 The Need for Early Notice of Infringement. Many a patent owner spends his funds amassing an impressive patent portfolio knowing that someday one or more of these patents will need to be asserted against a competitor. He may also police with care the activities of his competitors, watching for possible infringements. But despite these undertakings the patent owner is often unable to obtain recovery from a competitor for infringement activity that takes place undetected and therefore prior to the time when the patent owner notifies the competitor of the infringement. Significant amounts of royalties relating to early infringements by a competitor may be lost simply because the competitor has not been given timely notice of infringement.

7-2 Patent Marking. An extremely simple and inexpensive procedure that can be followed to prevent losses of royalties resulting from undetected infringements is called *patent marking*. Section 287 of Title 35 of the United States Code provides that if patentees and the persons making or selling any patented article for or under them will give notice to the public that the article is patented by either affixing thereon the term "patent" or the abbreviation "Pat." and the number of the patent, recovery can then be had relating to all infringement activities of a competitor. If one fails to mark one's products with a proper patent notice, one is precluded from recovering damages for infringements that have occurred prior to the time the competitor receives actual notice of infringement. For this reason, a patent owner should take care to see that he and his licensees use proper patent markings on all goods embodying the subject matter of a patent.

If a product incorporates the subject matter of more than one patent, a simple decal or label notice may be placed at a conspicuous location on the product stating that the product is covered by one or more patents and listing the patent numbers, together with a statement to the effect that other patents are pending, should this be the case.

7-3 False Marking. Just as proper patent marking is advantageous to a patentee, false patent marking can be detrimental. It is, in fact, a criminal offense punishable by a fine. Section 292 of Title 35 establishes a penalty of not more than $500 for each false patent marking offense.

Section 292 covers several types of false patent markings. It is illegal to knowingly mark unpatented goods as being patented, or to knowingly mark patented goods with the incorrect patent number. It is also illegal to knowingly mark an infringing product, produced without an appropriate patent license, with the number of another's patent because the purchasing public might thereby be deceived to believe that the product is made under a suitable patent license.

The penalty for false patent marking also applies to the use of such terms as "Patent Pending" and "Patent Applied For" in situations when no patent application has been filed or no patent application is still pending.

Proper product marking for compliance with other federal laws is discussed in Section 14-7.

7-4 Correction of Defects Through Reissue. If after a patent is issued, a patentee should discover a defect or insufficiency in the patent resulting from an inadvertent or accidental mistake, this person may surrender the original patent and apply for a reissue patent to correct the error.

For an error to be correctable through reissue, it must have arisen without deceptive intention. A patentee may not seek, by the route of reissue, to change the claims in an issued patent to recapture subject matter intentionally surrendered to obtain the original patent. Moreover, the reissue patent may not contain any new matter.

If a patentee seeks to enlarge by reissue the scope of the claims of the original patent, he must file a broadening reissue application within two years from the date of issuance of the original patent. If the patentee seeks to narrow his claims or otherwise correct some defect in a patent through reissue, other than enlarging the scope of the claims of the patent, he may file a narrowing reissue application at any time during the 17-year term of the patent.

7-5   Reexamination Through Reissue.   In 1978, the Patent and Trademark Office began permitting patentees to seek reexamination of patents through the route of reissue. This provision is of particular importance to patent owners anticipating the enforcement of their patents by litigation or who are already involved in such litigation. It is possible to file a reissue application and obtain an opinion from the Patent and Trademark Office on the validity of the patent in view of newly discovered prior art. This opinion can be used in guiding a court's interpretation of the patent's validity. However, the opinion is only advisory in nature and is not binding on any court.

If a reissue application is filed to obtain consideration of newly discovered art, and if the Patent and Trademark Office is of the opinion that the original patent is valid as it stands, no reissue patent will be issued. Instead, the file of the original patent will reflect the fact that the Patent and Trademark Office has considered and discounted the effect of the newly discovered art. In the event the Patent and Trademark Office believes the newly discovered art invalidates one or more of the claims of the original patent, or that amendment of one or more of its claims is needed, the file of the original patent will reflect these opinions. In this situation, a reissue patent will issue only if the patentee is successful in amending his claims so that the claims define an invention that is patentably distinguishable over the newly discovered art.

In many instances, a patentee who files a reissue application will do well to invite his adversaries to participate in the reissue proceeding. If the adversary does not participate, particularly when invited to do so, he may be subjected to criticism in future litigation should the patentee seek to enforce the resulting reissue patent. If an adversary does participate in a reissue proceeding, he does so from a position of disadvantage, in that he cannot initiate interviews or file appeals. He is limited to the filing of a protest.

7-6 Protest. While one is permitted to *protest* the issuance of a pending application, the Office has severely restricted the participation rights of protestors. To be considered by the Office, a protest must comply with requirements that call for a listing of references on which the protest is based, a concise statement of the relevance of each reference, a copy of each reference, and an English-language translation of all pertinent parts of foreign references.

With respect to an original application, all a protestor can do is to file his protest. He will receive a stamped postcard acknowledging its receipt if one was filed with the protest, but will not otherwise be permitted to participate in prosecution of the application. In a reissue case the protestor receives a notice of the entry of his protest in the file, but likewise cannot otherwise participate in the prosecution of the application.

7-7 Statutory Disclaimer. If a patentee discovers that one or more claims of his patent are invalid because they claim more than he was entitled to claim, this error can be rectified by filing a statutory disclaimer, a formal paper renouncing and dedicating to the public one or more of the claims in a patent.

Filing a statutory disclaimer is a much less involved procedure than is the filing of a reissue application. When a disclaimer is filed, no examination of the application is made by the Patent and Trademark Office; instead, the disclaimer is simply entered in the file of the patent.

If a patentee is aware of an invalid claim in a patent that he intends to enforce by litigation, it is important for him to file a disclaimer of the invalid claim prior to the initiation of litigation, else he will be barred by statute from recovering costs of the action.

7-8   Enforcing Patents Against Infringers.   Patent rights cannot be enforced against infringers until a patent has issued. Beginning on the very day of patent issuance, however, efforts can be set in motion to curtail infringements by others and/or to seek payments from others for use of the patented invention. Indeed, as has been pointed out with repeated emphasis, the entire thrust of a patent grant centers about its owner's *negative right to exclude others* from unauthorized use of the patented invention.

The law recognizes several types of patent infringements. *Direct infringement* involves the making, using, or selling, within the United States and during the term of patent, of the entirety of an invention defined by a claim of the patent. *Inducement of infringement* includes a number of activities by which one may intentionally cause, urge, encourage, or aid another to infringe a patent. *Contributory infringement* occurs when a person aids or abets direct infringement, as is set out in Section 271(c) of Title 35, which states:

> Whoever sells a component of a patented machine, manufacture, combination or composition, or a material or apparatus for use in practicing a patented process, constituting a material part of the invention, knowing the same to be especially made or especially adapted for use in an infringement of such patent, and not a staple article or commodity of commerce suitable for substantial non-infringing use, shall be liable as a contributory infringer.

In determining whether patent infringement exists, a principle called the "doctrine of equivalents" can be utilized to aid the patent owner. This doctrine essentially extends the scope of a patent to define as infringements such practices as may not be literally covered by the language of the claims of a patent, but which clearly are equivalent and fall within the purview of the patent.

A patent infringement suit can be brought only in a federal district court where either (a) the infringer does business and infringement is committed or (b) the infringer resides. The suit must be brought within a six year statute of limitations prescribed by Section 286 of Title 35. An infringement action is initiated by filing a written complaint with the clerk of the district court where suit is being brought. A copy of the complaint is served on the defendant by the court. During the suit, the plaintiff has the burden of establishing by competent evidence that the defendant's activities infringe the patent in question. In addition, the plaintiff must defend any charge raised by the defendant to the effect that the plaintiff's patent is invalid.

Patent infringement litigation should not be entered into without a thorough understanding of its risk and expense. Patent litigation is risky in that, on a nationwide average, only about 40% of the patents that are being litigated have their validity upheld. Actually a 40% survival rate is understandable in that if a contest is carried out (it takes two to have a contest), there is usually some arguable weakness in a patent that leads the accused infringer to believe he has a likelihood of prevailing.

Patent litigation is almost always expensive. Both the plaintiff and the defendant in a patent infringement case have to establish complex positions of fact and law. It is not unusual for both parties to a patent infringement suit to incur costs in excess of $100,000, especially if the case is tried through appeal. For this reason, patent infringement litigation may not be economical unless there is a market at stake that is considerably in excess of the anticipated costs of litigation.

For several reasons it may be desirable to sue an infringer. One obvious reason is to collect damages for past infringement and enjoin further infringement. In some instances, it is desirable to establish an aggressive reputation regarding the handling of patent infringements to deter others from infringing. Still other reasons for filing suit may be presented by the particular circumstances of a given situation.

It is helpful to reduce as many uncertainties as possible before filing suit. It is desirable to do everything one can prior to filing suit to establish whether infringement of the patent is actually taking place and can be proved. Likewise, it is desirable to conduct a validity study on the patent in question prior to filing suit to make certain the defendant will be unable to easily attack the patent's validity.

7-9   Defenses to Patent Enforcement.   Noninfringement is one of several traditional defenses an accused infringer can raise in his behalf. Three other substantive defenses are raised quite commonly in an effort to preclude enforcement of a patent. The first of these is the defense of patent invalidity. While a patent is presumed to be valid, a court will normally inquire into its validity if the defendant puts the issue in question. Arguments favoring invalidity can be based on a variety of grounds including lack of novelty of the invention, obviousness, or insufficient disclosure of the invention in the patent being asserted. The relatively stringent standard of "clear" and "convincing" evidence must be met in establishing patent invalidity in view of the presumption of validity that arises with patent issuance.

A second, commonly asserted defense is that the patent is unenforceable as a result of fraudulent procurement or inequitable conduct by the patentee before the Patent and Trademark Office. In the event the defendant can show by clear, unequivocal, and convincing evidence that a breach of the applicant's duty of candor has, through an intentional or grossly negligent misrepresentation or withholding of material fact, taken place, the patent may be rendered unenforceable and the patent owner subject to other liabilities. However, the type of showing required to establish fraud must exceed mere evidence of simple negligence, oversight, or erroneous judgment made in good faith.

Another commonly asserted defense is that of unenforceability due to so-called patent misuse and/or violation of the antitrust laws. If a patent owner has exploited the patent in an improper manner by violating the antitrust laws or by effectively extending the patent beyond its lawful scope, the courts will refrain from assisting the patent owner in remedying infringement until such time as the misuse is purged and its consequences dissipated. Specific acts that do not justify utilization of this defense are set out in Section 271(d) of Title 35, which states:

> No patent owner otherwise entitled to relief for infringement or contributory infringement of a patent shall be denied relief or deemed guilty of misuse or illegal extension of the patent right by reason of his having done one or more of the following: (1) derived revenue from acts which if performed by another without his consent would constitute contributory infringement of the patent; (2) licensed or authorized another to perform acts which if performed without his consent would constitute contributory infringement of the patent; (3) sought to enforce his patent rights against infringement or contributory infringement.

7-10   Uniformity in Patent-Related Decisions.   For many years, important issues of patent law have received conflicting treatment in the various circuit courts of appeal. Some circuits traditionally have been far more receptive to the enforcement of patents in infringement actions than have others of the circuits. This has resulted in forum shopping and in races to the courthouse. Patent owners have sought to have their cases heard in circuits that tend to uphold patents. Accused infringers have sought to have cases heard in circuits which disfavor patents and tend to find either noninfringement or patent invalidity.

At long last, appeals from all federal district court cases involving patents are being directed to a single appeals court to assure decision uniformity. The new Court of Appeals for the Federal Circuit, which began work as of October 1, 1982, not only assumed the responsibilities of its predecessor, the Court of Customs and Patent Appeals, but also the handling of appeals in patent-related cases from federal district courts throughout the country. While judges of the Court of Appeals for the Federal Circuit repeatedly point out the Court's wide-ranging responsibilities and object to the court's being referred to as "the patent court," one of the principal purposes for establishing this court was to put an end to the atrocious lack of uniformity in the handling of patent cases which has long presented serious obstacles of uncertainty in efforts to enforce patents against infringers.

7-11 Outcome of a Suit. If a patent owner is successful in prevailing in an infringement suit, he will recover such damages as he can prove to have suffered, but not less than a reasonable royalty. In some situations, the patent owner may succeed in recovering the total amount of profits that would have resulted from the additional increment of business he would have enjoyed were it not for the activities of the infringer. The prevailing patent owner normally recovers court costs. If the court should find that the infringement was willful and deliberate, the defendant may be ordered to pay the plaintiff's reasonable attorney's fees, but this award is rare. Should the court determine that the infringement has been flagrant and without any justification, it may award up to three times the damages actually found; however, such an award is extremely rare.

In the event the accused infringer wins the suit, he normally recovers little more than court costs. In some exceptional cases, particularly when the court considers the plaintiff's legal action an abuse of judicial process, the plaintiff may also be ordered to pay the defendant's reasonable attorney's fees.

7-12 Settling a Suit. Because of the expensive character of patent litigation, it is common for patent infringement suits to be settled before they come to trial. As discovery proceeds during the initial phases of patent infringement litigation, it is not uncommon for both sides to ascertain weaknesses in their positions and to note the desirability of settlement.

One point when settlements are commonly effected is before a suit has been filed. In this situation, the patent owner confronts the infringer with the facts of the infringement and a settlement is negotiated. Another time when settlement is commonly achieved is after there has been some initial discovery in a suit. By this time the positions of the parties have been clarified and each party can evaluate the other's position. A third point is after each side is ready to go to trial.

At this time, both sides clearly know the strengths and weaknesses of their cases and they each may be anxious to eliminate the cost of an actual courtroom confrontation.

7-13   Declaratory Judgment Actions.   In the event that one finds himself being accused of infringing another's patent or finds his business being threatened by a possible suit for alleged patent infringement, he may commence a suit in federal court to have the threatening patent declared invalid or not infringed. The Federal Declaratory Judgment Act passed in 1934 enables an alleged infringer to seize the initiative and become a plaintiff, rather than defendant, in a patent suit.

For a declaratory judgment action to succeed, the patent owner must actually have threatened to sue either the allegedly infringing manufacturer or his customers. An actual controversy must exist between the parties.

What one does in filing a declaratory judgment action is to seek a ruling from a federal court that he is not infringing a patent and/or that the patent is invalid. Filing such an action forces a patent owner who is threatening an alleged infringer or his customers to "put up or shut up." Accused infringers sometimes file such actions when it has become clear that they are going to be sued by a patent owner, for the first to file is usually able to select which of any available forums that is most convenient for his use and most inconvenient and expensive for use by his opponent.

7-14   Failure to Sue Infringers.   The laws of our country do not require that patent owners take any positive action whatsoever with respect to enforcing their patents. Many companies obtain patents and hold them defensively to preclude others from using certain inventions in the future, or as safeguards against the possibility of competitors patenting the same inventions. This practice is harmful to no one in that, as has been pointed out previously, patents do not take from the public anything that was already in the public domain, but rather expedite the disclosure to the public of new inventions that will come into the public domain on expiration of the patents. For many companies, the principal value of their patents lies in the defensive uses they make of them.

7-15 Voluntary Arbitration. Effective February 27, 1983, a change in the patent law as provided for voluntary arbitration by parties to a patent-related contract of a broad range of disputed patent-related issues, including questions of patent validity and infringement. Arbitration proceedings are private, and the resulting decision is final and binding. An award resulting from an arbitration is enforceable when notice of the award has been filed with the Commissioner of Patents and Trademarks.

Arbitration can offer significant advantages over litigation such as the speed with which a decision is reached, relatively lower cost, reduced likelihood of damage to ongoing business relationships, and the ability to select arbitrators who are experts in the technical area of the dispute. The American Arbitration Association has established an extensive set of rules to govern the arbitration of patent disputes.

If arbitration is to be provided as a means for resolving patent-related disputes stemming from a contract, the contract should include provisions that clearly express an intent to arbitrate, a description of what constitutes arbitratable issues, a recitation of the governing law, a designation of the place of any hearings, and a set of procedures for appointing arbitrators as well as a definition of the qualifications arbitrators must meet. Other provisions dealing with costs, awards, and the like should also be included.

7-16 Interferences. Although it seldom happens occasionally two inventors acting independently make the same or substantially the same invention at about the same time. When this happens and in the event the Patent and Trademark Office receives applications from both inventors for patents, a procedure called an *interference* is instituted for the purpose of determining priority of inventorship. The person the law regards as the first inventor will receive any patent that eventually issues.

Once an interference has been declared by the Patent and Trademark Office, a proceeding much like a lawsuit is begun. Each party seeks to prove his right to a patent and to establish the other's lack of right to the patent. An interference may be instituted even after a patent issues. It may be instituted by one who has an application pending wherein this person copies one or more claims of the issued patent to provoke an interference.

Interference proceedings are complex and technical. This area of patent practice is one in which reform would be welcomed by many patent practitioners.

Priority of invention will normally be awarded to the first inventor to reduce an invention to practice. This is because the act of invention is deemed not to have been completed until an invention has been conceived and reduced to practice. An exception to the reduction to practice rule arises when the first to conceive is not the first to reduce to practice, and when the first inventor to conceive has exercised reasonable diligence in reducing the invention to practice. When this exception applies, the period of diligence must extend from a time just before the second inventor began his activities, through the time of reduction to practice of the first inventory.

Since an interference can arise after a patent has issued, one must not destroy his records of early activities simply because a patent has issued.

CHAPTER EIGHT

Maintaining Proper Invention Records

The fact that one is the first inventor of an invention may not be sufficient to enable him to prevail in an interference priority contest unless evidence to prove his early conception is preserved. Other invention records are often needed to establish diligence in reducing the invention to practice. This chapter outlines preferred practices to be followed in preparing and preserving invention records.

8-1 Documenting Conception.   Ideally, the moment a new and useful invention is conceived, the inventor should at once prepare a written record, known as a disclosure, including a description and such sketches as are needed to fully describe what has been conceived. The disclosure should be made in ink and be signed and dated by the inventor. It should also be signed and dated by one or more witnesses who have reviewed the disclosure and to whom the full import of disclosure has been explained, preferably in confidence. If possible, the disclosure should be witnessed by at least two persons who fully understand its content. The endorsement of the witnesses should appear on each page of the disclosure, preferably at the bottom of each page and beneath the legend: "Explained to, read and understood by us, this _____ day of _____, 19____."

8-2 The Need for Witnesses.   It is important that witnesses sign and date all pages of a disclosure as this provides evidence that they actually read and understood each page. If a disclosure has been witnessed properly, it can be used to refresh the recollections of witnesses at a later date. Otherwise, should the witnesses be called to testify in a legal controversy, perhaps many years later, an opposing counsel may extract from the witnesses admissions that they do not actually remember reading the disclosure. If the signatures of the witnesses appear only on the last page, this may raise a question about whether they had read and understood the preceding pages.

The uncorroborated testimony of an inventor about a date of conception will not be accepted. While corroboration may be supplied, in some instances, by establishing appropriate circumstances surrounding that date, at least one witness is almost always essential.

The reason for having two or more witnesses sign a disclosure is to increase the probability of finding at least one witness who will be available when needed. Since written records are important evidence in an interference or in an infringement litigation, and since interference and litigation activities may take place many years after an invention has been conceived, common sense suggests that witnesses who are young and healthy may be more readily available years later when needed.

8-3 Disclosure Format. There is no specific requirement about the form a written disclosure must take to document the conception of an invention. Almost any form of evidence regarding conception may be helpful in the event it is needed. A disclosure functions chiefly to refresh the recollection of witnesses so that they can testify to the date they witnessed the disclosure. A dated and witnessed disclosure also serves to lend plausibility to the testimony of witnesses.

While inventors have been known to make disclosure records on the backs of envelopes, on shirt cardboards, and the like, this sort of informality is not to be encouraged. A far better practice is to establish a program for maintaining careful written records of all research and development work.

8-4 Use of Invention Notebooks. Written records of developmental activities are best maintained in bound notebooks. Many corporations provide their engineers and research workers with notebooks specifically designed for the recording of developmental activities. Daily entries are encouraged. Bound notebooks from which no pages can be removed and into which no pages may be inserted are vastly preferred. This type of book eliminates any possible question about whether pages have been removed or interleaved at a later date.

Each page in an invention notebook should be signed and witnessed in close proximity to the date of the entries on that page. Each entry in an invention notebook should be made in chronological order. Notebook pages should be consecutively numbered, with all entries made in ink. If an error is made in any entry, it should not be erased; it should be crossed out. If any portion of a page is left blank, it should be crossed out. No supplemental notes should be added to a page once that page has been signed and dated.

Invention notebooks can be purchased that have alternate pages perforated for removal so a carbon copy of each page can be made and removed for separate storage. All entries in an invention notebook should be made by the individual engineer in his own handwriting, not that of an assistant or secretary. Each person involved in a developmental project should be provided with a notebook of his own and should be instructed about the proper manner of recording thoughts and experiments.

As soon as an invention notebook is assigned to an engineer, he should write a few words on the inside cover of the notebook indicating that this particular notebook has been assigned to him. He should sign his name and date his signature. This procedure not only facilitates identification of the notebook, but also helps to establish the handwriting characteristics and signature of the inventor.

The value of entries made in an invention notebook is enhanced if they are in a form meaningful to others reading them at a later time. If a record of each experiment or test is prefaced with a brief statement of the purpose of the procedure, this will do much to explain the entries that follow. A further advantage of preparing a statement of purpose is that it may help the engineer crystallize his objectives and may therefore actually help him reach the desired solution.

Maintenance of laboratory notebooks in a systematic fashion not only provides a source of patent disclosures, but also affords a chronological record of activity that can be used to prove the fact that one has reduced an invention to practice and that one has proceeded diligently in doing this.

8-5   Preparing a Disclosure for a Patent Attorney.   Patent attorneys regularly are asked about the form in which a disclosure of an invention should be prepared for presentation to a patent attorney. Ideally, such a disclosure should be more complete and detailed than a laboratory notebook entry. The disclosure is preferably made in writing and accompanied by drawings or pictures as needed to provide the attorney with a relatively compact record to keep in the files.

The disclosure must be sufficiently clear to enable the patent attorney to understand the character of the invention being described. Ideally, the disclosure will be so clear and complete that it will enable an inexperienced individual to understand the basic thrust of the invention. The more complete the disclosure, the better are the inventor's prospects of obtaining thorough patent protection. The disclosure should be signed, dated, and witnessed in the manner described previously.

If the invention has actually been reduced to practice in the laboratory, or if a working model has been built and tested, the written disclosure should include a statement of these facts with notations of the dates on which reduction to practice was begun and completed. The names of the persons to whom the working invention was demonstrated and the dates of such demonstration should be provided in the disclosure. The date of conception of the invention should also be included, along with the names of any colleagues or witnesses who can corroborate it. If an initial disclosure was made as of the date of conception or if there are other available descriptive papers or blueprints, copies of these should be appended.

A properly signed, dated, and witnessed disclosure is far superior to the very questionable practice followed by some inventors who prepare a disclosure and mail it to themselves with the thought of preserving the sealed postmarked envelope bearing the disclosure. A sealed envelope can provide a subject of considerable curiosity to

children and others, and in the event any one of them decides to open
the envelope, the evidentiary value of the enclosed document is destroyed.

While patent attorneys are accustomed to accepting disclosures
from a client in almost any form, the ideal disclosure will take the
form of several permanently prepared pages, numbered consecutively, that present the full names and residence addresses of the inventors; a brief discussion of what each inventor has contributed; the
identity of the company or person who is to own the resulting patent;
the date information can be corroborated regarding conception and
reduction to practice; a listing of other drawings and other documents
where the invention is disclosed so reference can be made to this other information at a later time; a brief description of the most pertinent
prior art known to the inventors; a brief description of the problem of
the prior art; a summary about how the invention overcomes these
problems; a summary of what is believed to be novel; any pertinent
information, including dates, regarding activities that may have been
undertaken to make the invention public or to offer it for sale; and
such other information in the form of sketches, written descriptions,
photographs, and the like, as is needed to describe the invention so a
person skilled in the art can understand and practice it.

8-6 Documenting Diligence.   Should an interference proceeding
be instituted, it could be important to be able to establish that one has
been diligent in his efforts to reduce an invention to practice. In some
instances a delay of only a few days or weeks in attempting to reduce
an invention to practice may constitute a failure of diligence. In other
instances, depending on the reasons for a delay, a project may be set
aside for a number of years without interrupting the required chain of
diligence.

A party in an interference who has the later of two filing dates for
an application can win priority over the other party by proving that he
conceived an invention prior to the time of conception of the senior
party and that he acted with reasonable diligence in reducing his invention to practice. Alternatively, the junior party may win by show-

ing that, even though he conceived his invention at a time after the senior party's conception, he, the junior, actually reduced the invention to practice before the senior party filed his application and that the senior party was not diligent in filing his application after conceiving his invention. An inventor who is first to conceive and first to actually reduce to practice, but who keeps his invention secret for a substantial period of time prior to filing for patent protection will lose an interference with a later inventor who discloses the invention to the public by filing a patent application. Thus diligence is required not only in completing the invention, but also in filing for patent protection.

While the foregoing summary of how diligence may come into play may be confusing, the importance of being able to establish diligence should be apparent. The spirit of the patent law requires that an inventor complete his invention in a practical form and without unreasonable delay. An inventor may do so by actually reducing the invention to practice, in the form of a working embodiment, or by constructively reducing the invention to practice, as by the filing of a patent application.

In most instances when patent protection is pursued, a situation does not arise in which another inventor enters the field between the time the first inventor conceives an invention and reduces it to practice. Accordingly, in most instances, there will be no occasion for investigating the inventor's diligence, and delay on his part will not prejudice the validity of his patent. One can never be sure, however, that others are not working on the same problem, and for this reason, it is wise for all inventors to puruse diligently the completion and patenting of their inventions.

CHAPTER NINE

Planning a Patent Program

The majority of inventors in the United States today are employed by corporations engaged in research, development, or manufacturing. Since individual inventors do not ordinarily face the problem of managing a patent program, this chapter is directed primarily to those in corporate management who must make decisions of company patent policy. Some of the considerations that follow do apply to individual inventors, as well as to those creative people employed by others.

9-1 Knowing the Prior Art. The first consideration in establishing a patent program is to provide some means of becoming familiar with such prior art as in relevant to the inventor's or the company's major fields of interest. Much time and effort can be saved by knowing what has been done in the prior art so that one can initiate his efforts where others have left off. There is no substitute for knowledge and no excuse for not knowing what others have done in one's major areas of interest.

One way to become familiar with what has been done in the prior art is to have state-of-the-art searches conducted in these areas and to assemble collections of patents illustrating the work of others. Such searches will often disclose a surprisingly large number of patents presenting various solutions to problems of particular interest to the company. By reviewing prior patents one can ascertain what avenues have been explored and with what success. Often a thorough knowledge of what has been done before greatly assists in perceiving a better and heretofore untried approach.

9-2 Keeping Abreast of the Patent Activities of Others. As patents issue to competitors and as patents issue in specific fields of one's interest, copies of these patents should be systematically ordered and studied. This is important not only in keeping one abreast of the activities of others, but also in detecting possible infringement concerns that may be posed by these newly issued patents. A simple way of keeping abreast of the activities of others is to assign to a particular individual the responsibility of reviewing the *Official Gazette* of the Patent and Trademark Office. Each weekly issue of the *Official Gazette* presents synopses of the patents issued during a particular week.

Most patent attorneys maintain a subscription to the *Official Gazette* and are accustomed to spending time with each week's issue in an effort to locate patents of possible interest to their clients. I encourage my clients to give me a list of their competitors and other persons or entities whose patent activity would be of interest. This information is assembled in the form of a lengthy checklist that is used in reviewing the indices of each *Official Gazette* to compile a list of patents of interest to clients.

9-3   Avoiding Infringement.   When a company plans to introduce a new product, consideration should be given to the possibility that it might infringe existing patents. If any significant investment is involved in production tooling or if the product is one of particular importance to the company, a careful infringement study should be undertaken. Infringement studies are more extensive in scope than patentability studies and require that the claims of relevant active patents be reviewed carefully.

In some instances, patents may be found that arguably appear to cover the proposed new product. When this is the case, it is desirable to review the file histories of these troublesome patents to determine whether the language of the claims should be given a more restricted interpretation than might otherwise appear to be the case. Since patent applications normally include claims ranging in scope from broad to narrow, the fact that some of the claims of a patent are not infringed by the proposed product does not mean that all the claims of the patent are not infringed. In short, the claims of all patents that appear to have relevance to the new product must be examined with care.

If a patent is found that is infringed by the new product, several alternatives may be explored. The first possibility that should be considered is to modify the proposed product to conform precisely to a structure in the expired art. Since the teachings of an expired patent are available to all to use, these teachings cannot be covered by an unexpired, enforceable patent. When the product design has been so modified, the argument can be made that the product is in the public domain and cannot, therefore, be the subject of a valid infringement concern. This argument of noninfringement will prevail even though one or more claims of the troublesome patent may cover the modified product design.

A second option is to redesign the product so that it unquestionably avoids infringing the claims of the troublesome patent. This approach should offer protection against liability for infringement. On the other hand, patent claims are intended to be written in sufficiently broad language to cover almost any equivalent that performs substantially the same function. If one does succeed in designing around the infringed claims, the resulting product may be commercially impractical and/or may infringe yet another patent.

A third possibility is to conduct a validity study to determine whether the infringed patent is valid. Such a study should be initiated only after it has been determined that a patent is definitely infringed and that the infringed patent cannot be circumvented. A validity study is ordinarily of considerably broader scope than the examination search performed by the examiner before allowing the patent in question. Accordingly, while an exhaustive validity study can be costly, it may succeed in turning up prior art that invalidates the patent. The type of prior art needed to be found is the sort that will establish that what is claimed in the patent was old and unpatentable at the time of filing the application on which the patent is based.

Another option is simply to ignore the infringed patent hoping that the patent owner may never become aware of one's infringement activity or that the patent owner will not be sufficiently aggressive to prosecute patent infringement. This option does nothing to minimize one's exposure to liability and I certainly do not encourage it. As a practical matter, however, there are businesspersons who are willing to take calculated risks and who believe that, on occasion, the risk of ignoring a possible infringement concern may be justified. When a patent is about to expire and the activity one plans to undertake prior to the actual expiration date would be so minimal that a patentee would almost undoubtedly not pursue the infringement issue, ignoring an infringed patent is a risk some businesspersons are willing to assume.

Other possible alternatives include taking a license or acquiring all rights in the patent by outright purchase. Sometimes it is desirable to consider the possibility of purchasing the entity owning the troublesome patent. In some instances a company may be more receptive to an offer to purchase its entire assets than toward an offer to purchase one of its patents.

9-4 Protecting One's Own Developments.   A further element of any patent program is establishing a policy for protecting the fruits of the company's development programs. In this regard, a company should determine the degree of emphasis it wants to assign to the solicitation of patents. The determination of company patent policy is more a matter of business judgment than a legal decision. The advantages of building a portfolio of patents must be weighed against the costs and efforts required. Also to be considered are the exposure the company may suffer for failure to have protected its developments and the royalty income it may have failed to take in or be forced to pay out.

When a company is manufacturing products that can be copied by others, it is desirable to obtain a portfolio of patents that will deter copying by competitors and serve as trading stock in the event infringement concerns arise. Because a company may not have a large portfolio of patents does not necessarily mean that it has a small patent budget. If a company's products lie in areas of active development, it may be essential for the company to utilize a fairly substantial percentage of its patent budget checking each new development for possible infringement concerns.

Although a company may not be interested in licensing its developments, it should not avoid spending a reasonable amount of money for patent protection. Once a patent comes into existence, it is an asset in its own right and can significantly increase the worth of a company. Patents can be obtained and used advantageously for entirely defensive reasons, for example, to keep competitors from patenting one's developments. Maintaining a portfolio of patents may prove valuable in affording the company an opportunity to cross-license another in the event a suit for patent infringement is brought or the company wants to expand its product line to include the same general type of new product that has been patented by a competitor.

9-5   Encouraging Employee Development Contributions. A company's patent policy should include positive procedures for encouraging employees to contribute to the body of intellectual property owned by the company. Employees should be apprised of how they can submit ideas directly to the company's patent department or to a person or committee assigned to review these disclosures. Employee disclosures ought to be reviewed promptly and appropriate actions taken without delay. The company should in some way reward all useful contributions.

In many instances, management will find it beneficial to encourage submission of inventive ideas by adopting a suitable employee incentive plan. If a certain amount of prestige or professional advancement can be associated with helpful contributions, this alone may constitute a sufficient incentive.

9-6   Guarding Confidential Information. When a company's more valuable assets are its trade secrets, efforts should be undertaken to maintain strict confidentiality. Appropriate physical security arrangements should be taken to prevent outsiders from gaining access to secrets and to prevent those within a company who do not need to know confidential information from learning it. Visitor passes such as the one shown here may be utilized to impress on business visitors that any information they may learn during a plant visit is to be maintained in confidence.

Key employees, and consultants and suppliers should be required

No 3050

VISITOR

VISITOR'S NAME (PLEASE PRINT)

LICENSE NUMBER

REPRESENTING

ADDRESS (CITY & STATE)

TO SEE

ITEMS CARRIED:

☐ BRIEFCASE   ☐ SAMPLES

OTHER:

In consideration for the opportunity to visit the premises of Empigard Corporation, The Empire Plating Company, and/or Complete Coatings Corporation, hereinafter the "Empigard Companies," I hereby agree for myself and on behalf of my employer to keep confidential and will not disclose to anyone, the information concerning equipment design, manufacturing processes, or any other trade secrets, acquired through my visit at the Empigard Companies.

During my visit I understand that I am only permitted to enter production areas when escorted by authorized personnel, that the handling of equipment or materials is not permitted, unless I represent a Vendor servicing specific equipment for the Empigard Companies, and that taking photographs or making sketches or other reproductions is similarly prohibited.

Further, in consideration of being granted access to the Empigard Companies' premises, I agree to assume all risks of accident or injury during my visit, and I do hereby release the Empigard Companies from any claim for personal injury and/or property damage occurring on said premises, whether caused by the act of negligence of the Empigard Companies, or its employees, or otherwise.

I accept the foregoing conditions and acknowledge receipt of a copy of the Visitor Registration.

X

SIGNATURE   DATE

APPROVED BY

DATE & TIME

Empigard Corporation, 2820 E. 90th Street
The Empire Plating Company, 8800 Evarts Road
Complete Coatings Co., 9107 Frederick Ave.
CLEVELAND, OHIO

to sign agreements acknowledging their duties to hold in confidence the trade secrets of the company. Disclosures of confidential information to employees and one's manufacturer representatives should be made only after entering into suitable confidential disclosure agreements. The proprietary and confidential character of information given to suppliers in the form of drawings and requests for quotations can be emphasized by applying a suitable confidentiality notice to these documents in the following form:

Confidential Notice

This document and the designs, specifications, and engineering information disclosed hereon are the property of XYZ, Inc., and are not to be disseminated or reproduced without express written consent. This document is loaned in confidence and then only for review of the matter disclosed hereon. In consideration for the loan of this document and the opportunity to review its contents, the recipient agrees to keep it and the matter disclosed hereon in confidence and not to use nor permit their use in any way detrimental to XYZ, Inc.

A more complete discussion of trade secrets and their protection appears in Chapter 20.

CHAPTER TEN

Disclosing an Idea
and Invention Marketing

If it took nothing more than the actual act of inventing to make money from an invention, there would be many more wealthy people in this country. A great many people find that they have good, inventive ideas that others could use. In many instances, however, these people do not have the money or expertise to fund manufacture or to merchandise an inventive concept. They must therefore get financial support from others and/or enter into some sort of suitable licensing arrangement with others if economic advantage is to be obtained from their creative endeavors.

This chapter explores some of the pitfalls to avoid in seeking assistance from those who may be in a position to help. Also treated is the need a company has for establishing a program for the handling of ideas submitted from outsiders.

10-1 Preparing to Seek Assistance. In rare instances, an inventor's reputation alone may be enough to draw the necessary support from others. In the majority of situations, however, if one is to gain the support he needs from others, this support must be won based on a combination of the merit of the invention itself and the protection the inventor has obtained or is entitled to obtain.

To elicit needed support from others, it is often necessary for the inventor to take some initial steps on his own, involving an expenditure of his own funds. Ideally, the inventor will be able to fund a careful patentability study; assuming the results of that study are favorable, he would also ideally be able to fund the careful preparation and filing of a patent application. Having taken these basic steps, the inventor will have gained some insight into the scope of protection available for his invention and a description of the invention will have been generated in the form of the specification and drawings of a patent application.

The value a prospective backer or manufacturer may attribute to an outsider's idea will depend to an important degree on the scope of patent protection available. If an inventor has taken prudent steps to ascertain the scope of available patent protection and has initiated suitable efforts to pursue patent protection, the invention may be viewed in a far more favorable light than would otherwise be the case. Moreover, since those persons who may be interested in investing in an invention will be concerned about having its character defined as precisely as possible before they make an evaluation and an investment commitment, the existence of a document such as a patent application in which the character of the invention has been precisely described and illustrated will often do much to aid in the solicitation of outside assistance.

If one has not filed a patent application before the substance of his idea is published or offered for sale in a product embodying the idea, or if a patent application has not been filed before someone uses or permits another to use the idea except on a purely experimental basis, the idea can become unpatentable and available to everyone to use one year from the first date of any of these occurrences. Moreover, if a public disclosure of an idea takes place even one day before the filing of a U.S. patent application, this may make it impossible to obtain valid patent rights in many foreign countries.

10-2 Submitting an Idea to a Manufacturer.   When an inventor approaches a manufacturer with a new idea, both parties are concerned about being treated fairly. The inventor does not want the idea stolen and wants to be paid a fair price if the company decides to use the idea. Manufacturers, on the other hand, usually have a research and development program of their own underway. They do not want to be accused by an outsider of having stolen the outsider's idea when, in fact, the manufacturer may be about ready to market the idea after years of investment have been made to put the idea in a practical form.

By agreeing to review an idea received from an outsider, a company exposes itself to the possibility of being sued if the outsider should wrongfully come to believe that his idea has been stolen. On the other hand, by refusing to review a submitted idea, a company may be passing up a potentially valuable invention simply to avoid the risk of controversy. It is preferable for a company to acknowledge receipt of all unsolicited materials and, if it does not enter into confidential relationships with outside submitters, to so advise the submitter so that the submitter will be put on notice from the outset.

In some instances, an inventor may succeed in getting a company to receive his invention disclosure in confidence. In such situations, the company receiving the disclosure assumes an obligation to refrain from disclosing to others information the company receives, using the information, and assisting others to use it without some suitable arrangement having been entered into with the inventor. If an inventor can get a company to receive his disclosure in confidence, the recipient of the disclosure may thereafter be barred from using the idea unless the recipient pays for it. This obligation may be enforceable even though the subject matter of the disclosure may not be patentable.

It may not be possible to persuade a company to agree to receive a disclosure on a confidential basis. When that is the case, the inventor must give up his right to have his idea reviewed in confidence to get the idea reviewed at all. Under these circumstances, if an inventor desires legal protection against the possible theft of his disclosure, he must rely solely on his rights under the patent law.

Because companies are acutely aware of the unfortunate consequences that can arise when invention disclosures are received from outside individuals, some companies have adopted the policy of flatly refusing to receive any submitted ideas from outside, whether submitted on a confidential basis or otherwise. Other companies will consider submitted ideas from outsiders only after the inventor has filed a patent application, the understanding being that the inventor's right to recovery for use of the invention shall be solely under the patent laws.

Probably the most common practice used by companies in handling submitted ideas is to require the inventor to first sign an agreement limiting the company's liability for consideration of the disclosure. Submitted idea agreements of this type usually emphasize that the idea is not being recieved under any sort of confidential relationship. Many of these agreements indicate that if the idea is not patentable, but is nevertheless new and original, and the company wishes to use the idea, the company alone will determine the amount of money to be paid to the inventor. Another common provision in these agreements is that if a valid patent has been, or can be, obtained on the invention and the company wishes to use the invention, the company will then negotiate with the inventor for the right to make, use, and/or sell the invention. A provision used by some companies in their submission review agreements gives the company the *exclusive* right, typically for a period of three months, to work out an agreement with the inventor for *exclusive* use of the invention. Such a provision benefits the company far more than the inventor.

10-3   Invention Marketing Firms.   As almost every inventor is aware, many invention marketing companies purport to assist inventors in marketing ideas. In recent years approximately 250 of these companies have been known to exist. They reportedly constitute a $100 million a year business.

Unfortunately, the majority of inventors who have had dealings with these companies have received little of value in return for the money they have paid. Investigations by the Federal Trade Commission and others have found widespread deceptive practices.

I have counseled several clients who have been served by invention marketing companies. In one instance, an inventor had approached an invention marketing company that had assisted him, through the services of a patent agent, in having a patentability search performed and a patent application filed. The search failed to turn up any art having reasonable relevance to the invention. Accordingly, the inventor's hopes were greatly bolstered, and he gladly funded the suggested preparation and filing of a patent application. Unknown to the inventor, when the resulting patent application was filed, it disclosed a totally inoperable invention. The parts of the invention that needed to be movable to function were either shown in the drawing as being formed integrally or as being welded together. The application was rejected by the Patent and Trademark Office when an initial search performed by an examiner uncoverd a very substantial body of pertinent art, none of which had been found during the search for which the inventor had paid.

In other instances, I have counseled clients who have disclosed their inventions in confidence to invention marketing companies and who have been assisted by the companies in the filing in the Patent and Trademark Office of Disclosure Documents. Since the Patent and Trademark Office will retain a Disclosure Document for a period of two years, the clients in these instances had wrongfully assumed that they had a two-year grace period during which to file patent applications without possible loss of benefits. This is incorrect. Once the invention marketing companies had prepared discloures and published them in an effort to find investors, purchasers, or licensees for the inventions involved, the inventors then had only a year's time to file patent applications. By the time they deemed it appropriate to visit a patent attorney, these one-year periods had long since expired and the inventors' patent rights had been dedicated to the public.

While I do not wish to suggest that no reputable invention marketing companies exist, my own experience, along with the experiences of other patent attorneys who have counseled former clients of invention brokers, has been that many of these clients were not well served by the invention brokers. The reputation of invention marketing companies as a whole clearly leaves something to be desired.

For those who would like something more extensive to read on the subject of invention marketing, an informative booklet entitled "How to Protect and Benefit from Your Ideas" may be purchased at a nominal price from the American Patent Law Association, 2001 Jefferson Davis Highway, Arlington, VA 22202, (703) 521-1680.

10-4   Disclosure Documents.   In accordance with the Disclosure Discount Program, an inventor may deposit with the Patent and Trademark Office a paper disclosing an invention. The purpose of this program is to assist inventors in documenting the conception dates of their inventions. While there are no restrictions regarding the content of such a document, it must be limited to written matter or drawings and should provide a full disclosure of the invention. Photographs may be included if they aid in understanding the disclosure.

A fee is charged for the filing of a disclosure document. The document must be submitted in duplicate and accompanied by a stamped, self-addressed envelope and a separate transmittal paper in duplicate, signed by the inventor, stating that he is the inventor and requesting that the material be received for processing under the Disclosure Document Program. On receipt by the Office, these papers will be date-stamped and assigned an identifying number. The duplicate papers will be returned in the self-addressed envelope, together with a warning to the inventor that the disclosoure document may be relied on only as evidence of conception of an invention.

The Office will preserve a disclosure document for a period of two years. At the end of the two-year period, disclosure documents are destroyed unless they are referred to in a separate letter in a related patent application filed within the two-year period. No reference to a disclosure document need be made in a patent application if the inventor does not want the Patent and Trademark Office to retain the disclosure document beyond the two year period.

The Disclosure Document Program unquestionably constitutes a suitable manner in which one can document invention dates; however, many patent attorneys are concerned that this program may have done more harm than good. Keeping careful invention records that are dated and witnessed by others is an entirely acceptable way of documenting invention dates. Accordingly, the Disclosure Document Program is not essential from this viewpoint. The problem with the program is that many inventors not familiar with the workings of our patent system are misled into thinking that they have taken the appropriate steps to procure a patent. More than one new client has visited my office seeking to sue a competitor for patent infringement based on a "patent" he purportedly obtained through the Disclosure Document Program. It cannot be overemphasized that absolutely no enforceable protection of any kind results from the filing of a disclosure document.

CHAPTER ELEVEN

Assignments, Shoprights, and Licenses

This chapter deals with various occurrences that cause some or all the rights in an invention to be transferred from one individual or company to another.

11-1 Assignments in General.   An assignment is a transfer of ownership rights with regard to a patent and the invention covered by the patent. It usually takes the form of a written document that includes the right to patent the invention, along with all rights in all patent applications and patents emanating from the invention. Often it is desirable in drafting an assignment to include a number of specific rights that transfer together with the patent, such as the right to sue for past infringements. If a pending United States application is being assigned, it may be desirable to include in the assignment a specific recitation of the right to file abroad claiming the benefit of the filing date of the United States application. An assignment is, in essence, a sale of an invention.

Section 261 of the Patent Act of 1952 provides that patents are "assignable in law by an instrument in writing." A patent assignment should be acknowledged before a notary public or other person authorized to administer oaths.

Patent law also provides a means for recording assignment documents in the Patent and Trademark Office on payment of a recordal fee. The law indicates that "an assignment . . . shall be void as against any subsequent purchaser or mortgagee for a valuable consideration, without notice, unless it is recorded in the Patent and Trademark Office within three months from its date or prior to the date of such subsequent purchase or mortgage." To maximize one's protection, it is desirable that an assignment of either a patent application or a patent be recorded promptly in the Patent and Trademark Office.

The practice followed by a few patent attorneys of waiting to record an assignment until an application has been allowed by the Office (purportedly to save the cost of a relatively small assignment recordal fee in the event the application does not issue as a patent) is a disservice to clients. This practice is undesirable not only from the viewpoint that the assignment document might be lost before it has been recorded, but also because waiting beyond three months to record the document could jeopardize the client's rights should the inventor execute another assignment to a good faith purchaser who proceeds promptly and in good faith to record his assigned rights.

11-2   Employee Agreement Assigning Invention Rights.   When an employee is employed under an agreement giving the employer all rights in inventions developed by the employee, it is common for an assignment document to be executed concurrently with the execution of a patent application and for the assignment document to be forwarded to the Patent and Trademark Office concurrently with the application. The assignment document is then recorded by the Office and is returned to the assignee for safekeeping.

In larger corporations, corporate patent policy includes a requirement that all key employees sign invention agreements giving their employer all rights to any inventions they may make during their employment. In smaller corporations and partnerships, a difficult situation sometimes occurs when officers of the corporation or members of the executive staff do not have employee agreements and, for reasons personal to the individuals involved, may not assign rights in patent applications to the company. Situations of this type are to be discouraged in view of the many problems that may arise should these key people leave the company.

It is desirable, wherever possible, to eliminate any conflict between employer and employee over invention ownership by providing an express agreement, in the form of an employment contract, defining in advance the ownership of rights to any inventions made by the employee. The minimum obligation normally presented in an employee invention agreement is one requiring that all inventions and any patents emanating from the work done by the employee on behalf of the company be assigned to the company.

Many employee agreements include within the domain of inventions assigned to an employer even those inventions not specifically related to the work assignments of the employee. Inventions unrelated to one's work developed on personal time and using solely the resources of the employee also may be included. Moreover, some employment contracts include obligations that extend a year or more beyond the term of the employee's employment to compel assignment of any inventions relating to the business of the employer. While agreements of these types are generally enforceable, the court will usually look at the reasonableness of the provisions in question.

Most companies will be willing to grant a release to an employee on an invention the company has no interest in exploiting. Obtaining a release is usually a relatively uncomplicated procedure involving far less employer-employee trauma than the employee may anticipate.

11-3   Prosecution of Application by Assignee.   Once an assignment has been made of the entire interest in a patent application, the assignee may intervene in the prosecution of the application and appoint an attorney of his own choice to handle prosecution. Such intervention does not, however, exclude the applicant from access to the application unless the assignee makes a specific request that the applicant be excluded. Even when such a specific request is made, the applicant may still be permitted to inspect the file of an application on suffficient showing of why an inspection is necessary to preserve his rights.

Only the assignee of the entire interest can intervene in the prosecution of an application to the exclusion of the applicant. An assignee of a part interest has no right to intervene, but is entitled to inspect the file of the application.

11-4 Issuance of Assigned Patent to Assignee.   When an assignment of the entire interest in a patent application has been made, the patent will normally issue to the assignee of record. If the assignee should hold a part interest, the patent will normally issue jointly to the inventor and the assignee. If it is desired that a patent issue to an assignee, an assignment document reflecting the assignee's interest must be recorded no later than the date payment is made of the issue fee. Irrespective of assignee participation in the prosecution of an application, the resulting patent will issue to the assignee of record.

11-5 Shoprights.   A *shopright* is a form of implied license. It is an irrevocable, nonexclusive, nontransferable, royalty-free license to an employer to use an employee's invention in the employer's own shop or factory throughout the life of any patent that may be granted to the employee. A shopright arises when an employee has made an invention using the time, materials, tools, or other resources of the employer.

Shoprights exist only in the absence of any express agreement defining the ownership of an invention made by the employee during the course of employment. Questions of shoprights most often arise when an invention is made by an employee who is not expected to make inventions and who has not been hired for that purpose. In such instances, the invention and any patent that may be obtained thereon usually belong to the employee, and the employer is entitled only to a shopright. Ordinarily no shopright arises where an employer requests and receives reimbursement from an employee for such time, materials, tools, or other employer-owned resources as were used by the employee in developing an invention.

11-6 Licenses in General.   A license is a permission, usually in written form, granted by the owner of certain rights permitting another entity to use some or all of those rights. A license usually is granted in exchange for royalty income, property, a cross-license, or something else of value.

The most common form of a patent license is a nonexclusive license. "Nonexclusive" means the patent owner reserves the right to grant licenses to others. If a patent owner grants an exclusive license, he cannot license others at a later time. An exclusive license usually costs more than a nonexclusive license since it forecloses the licensor's right to license others and assures the absence of head-to-head competition.

A danger to the patent owner in granting an exclusive license is that the licensee may shelve the invention or otherwise not pursue its practice as diligently as the licensor would like. Accordingly, it is prudent to include in an exclusive license appropriate performance terms providing that if the licensee fails to practice the invention to a reasonable degree, either the exclusive nature of the license may be withdrawn or the entire license agreement may be terminated at the option of the licensor.

While license agreements do not have to be recorded in the Patent and Trademark Office, it is in the interest of an exlcusive licensee to record his license as a protection against the possibility of someone else taking a license in good faith under the same patent.

11-7   Licenses and the Antitrust Laws.   A patent may be thought of as constituting a bundle of rights. This bundle of rights includes the right to exclude others from making, using, and selling the invention. Moreover, each of these rights includes other distinct rights. For example, the right to exclude others from making an invention includes the right to exclude others from making the invention in separate geographic areas of the United States. Similarly, the right to exclude others from using an invention includes the right to exclude others from using the invention for different purposes.

Common sense and logic would suggest that since a patent includes a bundle of individual and separable rights, it should be possible to license others under one or more of these rights without necessarily granting a license under all the rights. Thankfully, common sense prevails with regard to the licenseability of many of the various rights included within a patent owner's bundle. As antitrust laws are interpreted more and more stringently, however, the freedom of patent owners to license selected rights is diminishing. Since this is a changing area of law, particular attention needs to be paid in the drafting of license agreements not only to the current status of the law, but also to its trends.

The antitrust laws strictly prohibit one from requiring a licensee to pay royalties beyond the term of a licensed patent. A licensee may not be required to take a license under a plurality of patents to obtain a license under a particular patent of interest. A licensee may not be required to purchase an unpatented staple article of commerce from the licensor to receive a license. These are only a few of the prohibitions prescribed by antitrust concerns. There are many more.

11-8   Typical License Provisions.   A patent license agreement is ordinarily a relatively lengthy document, including provisions that treat a wide variety of possibilities which may arise during the term of the agreement. A patent license should include provisons that clearly, accurately and completely record the understandings of the parties to the agreement. The job of the attorney who drafts a license is to carry out his charge with precision, avoiding inconsistencies in language and uncertainties arising from a poor choice of words. While a license should include many customary provisions, they should all be couched in language of definite meaning.

One of these provisions addresses how royalty payments are to be made to the licensor. A single lump sum payment for a paid-up license may be used. Periodic payments of a fixed amount may be required. A fixed amount per unit; a percentage of gross sales, net sales after expenses, or profits; or of some other suitable revenue figure may be prescribed. Minimum annual payments may be required. Almost any reasonable payment arrangement that does not extend beyond the life of the licensed patent may be decided on by the parties to the agreement.

Another matter commonly treated in a license agreement is whether the licensee can grant sublicenses to others. Since sublicensees might be able to exploit areas of the marketplace that a licensee is unable to exploit, significant advantages may result from giving one's licensee the right to sublicense others. A problem that may result from granting sublicensing privileges is that the license may select sublicensees not as desirable as the patent owner would like. Bookkeeping and efforts to supervise quality control may be complicated by the existence of sublicensees who deal only indirectly with the patent owner through a licensee. In short, the granting of the right to sublicense others is something that must be considered carefully.

In some situations it may be desirable to give an exclusive licensee the right to sublicense others without requiring the exclusive licensee to consult with the licensor. This right is sometimes granted to avoid possible antitrust concerns based on a purported conspiracy between the licensor and the exclusive licensee.

11-9 Covenants Not to Sue.   A possible alternative to the granting of a license is to agree with a prospective licensee that he will not be sued for patent infringement so long as royalty payments are made. Such an agreement is called a covenant not to sue. An agreement of this type assures the grantee that the grantor will not bring any cause of action against the grantee except for nonpayment of royalties. In return for such an agreement, the grantee agrees to make periodic payments based on the success he achieves in practicing the invention.

In some instances, there are advantages to be had in characterizing an agreement between two parties as an assignment, a license, or a covenant not to sue. For example, an agreement may have different tax consequences for the parties involved, depending on how it is drafted.

CHAPTER TWELVE

Patent Protection
Available Abroad

United States patents provide no protection abroad and can be asserted against a foreigner only in the event the foreigner's activities infringe within the geographical bounds of our country. This chapter briefly outlines some of the factors one should consider if patent protection outside the United States is desired.

12-1 Canadian Filing. Many United States inventors file in Canada. Filing an application in Canada is relatively inexpensive compared with the cost of filing in other countries. With the exception of a stringently enforced unity requirement, which necessitates that all the claims in an application strictly define a single inventive concept, Canadian patent practice essentially parallels that of the United States. If one has success in prosecuting an application in the United States it is not unusual for the Canadian Patent Office to agree to allow claims of substantially the same scope as those allowed in the United States.

12-2 Foreign Filing in Other Countries. Obtaining foreign patent protection in countries other than Canada, particularly in non-English speaking countries, has long been an expensive undertaking. In almost all foreign countries, local agents or attorneys must be employed, and the requirements of the laws of each country must be met. Some countries exempt large areas of subject matter such as pharmaceuticals from what may be patented. It may be necessary to provide a certified copy of the United States case for filing in each foreign country selected. Translations are needed in most non-English speaking countries. In such countries as Japan, even the retyping of a patent application to put it in proper form can be costly.

With the exception of a few English-speaking countries, it is not at all uncommon for the cost of filing an application in a single foreign country to equal, if not exceed, the total costs that have been incurred in the entire process of preparing and filing the original United States application. These seemingly unreasonably high costs prevail even though the United States application, from which a foreign application is prepared, already presents the essential elements of the foreign case.

12-3   Annual Maintenance Taxes and Working Requirements.   In many foreign countries, annual fees are charged to maintain the active status of a patent. In some countries, the fees escalate each year on the theory that the invention covered by the patent must be worth more as it is put into practice more extensively. These annual maintenance fees not only benefit foreign economies, but also cause many patent owners to dedicate their foreign invention rights to the public. Maintaining patents in force in several foreign countries is often unjustifiably expensive.

In many foreign countries there are requirements that an invention be "worked" or practiced within these countries if patents within these countries are to remain active. Licensing a citizen of the country to practice an invention satisfies the working requirement in some countries.

12-4   Filing Under International Convention.   If applications are filed abroad within one year of the filing date of an earlier-filed United States case, the benefit of the filing date of the earlier-filed United States case may be attributed to the foreign applications. Filing within one year of the filing date of a United States case is known as filing under international convention. The convention referred to is the Paris Convention, which has been ratified by our country and by almost all other major countries.

Many foreign countries do not provide the one-year grace period afforded by United States statute to file an application. Instead, certain foreign countries require that an invention be "absolutely novel" at the time of filing of a patent application in these countries. If the United States application has been filed prior to any public disclosure of an invention, the absolute novelty requirements of certain foreign countries can be met by filing applications in these countries under international convention, whereby the effective filing date of the foreign cases is the same as that of the United States case.

12-5   Filing on a Country-by-Country Basis.   If one decides to file abroad, one approach is to file separate applications in each selected country. Most United States patent attorneys have associates in foreign countries with whom they work in pursuing patent protections abroad. It is customary for the United States attorney to advise a foreign associate about how he believes the prosecution of an application should be handled, but to leave final decisions to the expertise of the foreign associate.

12-6   The Patent Cooperation Treaty.   Since June 1978, United States applicants have been able to file an application in the United States Patent and Trademark Office in accordance with the terms of the Patent Cooperation Treaty (PCT), which has been ratified by the United States. While PCT member countries are becoming quite numerous, the use that has been made to date of PCT filings has been relatively minimal. Only about 5000 PCT applications are being filed worldwide each year. Only about 1800 PCT cases are being filed in the United States each year.

   PCT member countries include such major countries as Australia, Austria, Belgium, Brazil, Denmark, Finland, France, Hungary, the Netherlands, Norway, Sweden, the Soviet Union, Switzerland, the United Kingdom, the United States, West Germany, and others. In filing a PCT case, a United States applicant can designate the application for eventual filing in the national offices of such other countries as have ratified the treaty.

   One advantage of PCT filing is that the applicant is afforded an additional eight months beyond the one-year period he would otherwise have had under the Paris Convention to decide whether or not he wants to complete filings in the countries he has designated. Under the Patent Cooperation Treaty, an applicant has 20 months from the filing date of the United States application to make the final foreign filing decision.

Another advantage of PCT filing is that it can be carried out literally at the last minute of the one year convention period, measured from the date of filing of a U.S. application. Thus, in situations where a decision to effect filings abroad of separate applications in individual countries has been postponed until it is impractical if not impossible to implement, a single PCT case can be filed on a timely basis in the U.S. Patent and Trademark Office designating the desired countries.

Still another feature of PCT filing is that, by the time the applicant must decide on whether to complete filings in designated countries, he has the benefit of the preliminary search report (a first Office Action) on which to base his decision. If the applicant had elected instead to file applications on a country-by-country basis under international convention, it is possible that he might not have received a first Office Action from the Patent and Trademark Office within the one year permitted for filing under international convention.

12-7   The European Patent Convention.   Another option available to United States citizens since June 1978, is to file a single patent application to obtain protection in one or more of the European countries that are parties to the so-called European Patent Convention (EPC). It should be noted that the EPC is a convention separate and apart from the Common Market, with EPC membership not including all Common Market countries, yet including some countries that do not belong to the Common Market. As of this writing, EPC member countries include Austria, Belgium, France, Italy, Liechtenstein, Luxembourg, the Netherlands, Sweden, Switzerland, the United Kingdom, and West Germany.

Two routes are available to United States citizens to effect EPC filing. One is to act directly through a European patent agent or attorney. The other is to use PCT filing through the United States Patent and Trademark Office and to designate EPC filing as a "selected country."

A European Patent Office has been set up in Munich, West Germany. Before applications are examined by the EPO in Munich, a Receiving Section located at The Hague inspects newly filed applications for form. A novelty search report on the state of the art is provided by the International Patent Institute at The Hague. Within 18 months of filing, The Hague will publish an application to seek views on patentability from interested parties. Once publication has been made and the examination fee has been paid by the applicant, examination moves to Munich where a determination is made of patentability, and prosecution is carried out with the applicant responding to objections received from the examiner. The EPO decides whether a patent will issue, after which time a copy of the patent application is transferred to the individual patent offices of the countries designated by the applicant. The effect of EPC filing is that, while only a single initial application need be filed and prosecuted, in the end, separate and distinct patents issue in the designated countries. Any resulting patents have terms of 20 years measured from the date of filing of the original application.

12-8   Advantages and Disadvantages of International Filing.   An advantage of both PCT and EPC filing is that the required applications can be prepared in exactly the same format. Their form and content will be accepted in all countries that have adhered to the EPC and/or PCT programs. Therefore, the expense of producing applications in several different formats and in different languages is eliminated. The fact that both PCT and EPC applications can, in their initial stages, be prepared and prosecuted in the English language is another important advantage for United States citizens.

A principal disadvantage of both of these types of international patent filings is their cost. Before savings over the country-by-country approach are achieved, filing must be anticipated in several countries, perhaps as many as four to six, depending on which countries are selected. A disadvantage of EPC filing is that a single examination takes place for all the designated countries, and patent protection in all these countries is determined through this single examination procedure.

12-9   Trends in International Patent Protection.   With the advent of the PCT and EPC programs, a significant step forward has been taken that may someday lead to the development of a multinational patent system. For the predictable future, however, it seems clear that the major countries of the world intend to maintain intact their own patent systems. Certainly, the United States is reluctant to give full faith and credit to foreign patents in which foreign nationals would be permitted to enforce patents obtained in their countries in the United States. Similarly, other nations are reluctant to give United States citizens the right to exclude others from making, using, or selling inventions in their countries based solely on the issuance of patents in our country.

REFERENCES

Arnold, Tom, and Frank S. Vaden, III, *Invention Protection,* Barnes & Noble, New York, 1971.

Buckles, Robert A., *Ideas, Inventions and Patents*, Wiley, New York, 1957.

Chisum, Donald S., *Patents,* Matthew Bender, New York, 1978, 1983.

Kitner, Earl W., and Jack Lahr, *An Intellectual Property Law Primer,* Clark Boardman, New York, 2nd Ed., 1982.

Manual of Patent Examining Procedure, Government Printing Office, 4th Ed., June 1979, latest rev. Sept. 1982.

Mayers, Harry R., *Drafting Patent License Agreements,* Bureau of National Affairs, Washington, D.C., 1971.

Rosenberg, Peter D., *Patent Law Fundamentals,* Clark Boardman, New York, 1975.

Schramm, Frederic B., *Handbook on Patent Disputes,* Harrison, Atlanta, 1974.

White, Robert A., Rodney K. Caldwell, and John F. Lynch, *Patent Litigation: Procedure and Tactics,* Matthew Bender, New York, 1978.

PART THREE

TRADEMARKS

CHAPTER THIRTEEN

Basic Features of Trademarks

A *trademark* is any word, name, symbol, configuration, device, or any combination thereof one adopts and uses to identify and distinguish his goods or services from those of others. In essence, a trademark is a brand name or symbol utilized by a consumer to choose among competing goods or services. If you find something you like or dislike about a product or service, its trademark is what you recall in deciding whether to buy it again.

All our states have statutes dealing with trademarks. Federal law on the subject of trademarks is principally embodied in the Lanham Act.

13-1 Relationship to Unfair Competition. The right to use a trademark is one of the exclusive rights included in the general category of intellectual property. While patents and copyrights find a basis for their existence in our Constitution, no such constitutional basis gives rise to trademark protection. Trademark law is, instead, a part of the much broader common law of unfair competition.

Unfair competition is considered to be present when the activities of a competitor result in a likelihood of consumer confusion. Trademark infringement constitutes a particular type of unfair competition in which the activities of one's competitor are resulting in a likelihood of confusion in the minds of the buying public, and these activities relate to exclusive rights an owner has established in his trademark.

13-2 Relationship to Monopolies. Some people view trademarks through "monopoly-colored" glasses and thereby see evil in this

117

highly respected form of intellectual property. Indeed a misapplication of the term "monopoly" has presented a stumbling block for centuries to the protection of trademarks. Trademarks have been said to provide gifts of exclusive ownership in words and to create lawful monopolies immune from competition. A more accurate view is that a trademark establishes, for one who has adopted it, the legal right to prevent others from using the same or similar mark in a manner that presents a likelihood of confusion to buyers. In this sense, the trademark owner has an exclusive right, namely, to prevent others from creating a likelihood of confusion.

A trademark that has a great deal of goodwill associated with it may draw a great deal of customer loyalty, but this is not a monopoly situation. When a valuable reputation has been established in conjunction with the use of a mark, the salability of products or services associated with the mark is greatly enhanced.

By providing in our legal system a means for registering, protecting, and enforcing the trademark rights of others, we secure to ourselves the rights to not be misled and deceived by those who would trade on the good names of others. Enforcement of trademark rights is just as much in the interest of the consumer as it is in those who own the rights being enforced. Every time a trademark proprietor pursues an infringer he not only protects his own monetary interest but also acts to protect the public from being misled and deceived. Those who fail to see this important truth should be sentenced to live in a totally generic world of plain brown wrappers, using no brand name products or services. In such a world there is no incentive for excellence. Indeed, to the degree that competition would exist at all, it would lie solely in the effort to produce goods and services of the lowest possible quality because doing that is the cheapest thing to do, and no one would know against whom to retaliate.

As if it were not enough that trademarks have been so mistakenly confused with the term "monopoly," our courts have recently seen fit to strike down as no longer being entitled to trademark status the very valuable mark *Monopoly* for games. Whereas a trademark is not a monopoly, *Monopoly* was most certainly a fine trademark. To the deep regret of many, the Supreme Court declined the request made to review this unfortunate circuit court case.

13-3   Relationship to Patents.   A trademark is not patentable. Patents are granted on advances in the useful arts, not on symbols, words, or devices that identify and distinguish goods or services. While trademark rights may be generated in a particular type of article configuration, such as a perfume bottle, and while design patent protection may be had on the artistic and ornamental appearance of such an article, these two types of protections are different. A design patent will be infringed by one who produces articles of the same configuration, regardless of the use to which they may be put and regardless of whether a likelihood of confusion results. A trademark will be infringed only if another adopts and uses the same or similar configuration in connection with such goods as will cause a likelihood of confusion.

Patents and trademarks give their respective owners different kinds of rights. A patent gives its owner the right to exclude others from making, using, or selling a particular invention. A trademark gives its owner the right to exclude others from using the same or similar marks in a way likely to cause confusion or deception among customers.

The subject matter of a patent must be new, nonobvious, and original with the patentee. No such requirements exist with respect to trademarks. The subject matter of a patent need not be put into practice for a patent to be enforced; that is, patent rights exist entirely independently from invention use. A trademark, on the other hand, must be used continually or one's rights in it become abandoned.

A patent extends for a limited number of years. Rights in a trademark depend on use; they may subsist forever if appropriate use is continued.

13-4   Relationship to Copyrights.   An author can use his copyright to prevent others from copying his work. A trademark owner can prevent use by another entity of the same or a similar mark on such goods or services as are likely to cause confusion.

A trademark generally cannot be copyrighted. The label on which a trademark appears can be copyrighted so long as it presents original printed matter, but a brand name cannot, in and of itself, be protected by copyright.

Like patents, copyrights are required by the Constitution to be granted for "limited times." Trademarks, however, are not "writings" or "discoveries" as these terms are used in the Constitution, and properly can be preserved indefinitely for exclusive use by their owners.

13-5   Relationship to Trade Names.   *Trade names* are words or symbols used to distinguish companies, partnerships, and other business entities, as opposed to marks that are used to identify and distinguish goods and services.

There is no federal registration provision for trade names per se. If a trade name is used as a trademark, it may be registered federally and with the several states as a trademark. Most states have provisions for registrations of trade names. In some states, trade name registration is mandatory as a form of consumer protection to assure that those who do business cannot hide behind a trade name that fails to identify these businesspersons.

13-6   Types of Trademarks.   The term *trademark* is used not only to include what are technically defined as trademarks, but also to include what are known as service marks, certification marks, and collective marks. Technically, *trademarks* are marks used to distinguish one's goods from those of another. *Service marks* are marks used in the sale or advertising of services. *Certification marks* are marks used on, or in connection with, the products or services of one or more persons, other than the owner of the mark, to certify certain characteristics of the goods or services. *Collective marks* are marks used by members of a cooperative, an association, or other collective group or organization to indicate membership.

13-7   A Symbol of Goodwill.   A trademark is, in a sense, a repository of goodwill. It is a medium through which goodwill is made known to the public.

Just as patents and copyrights are linked inseparably to the existence of inventions and tangible mediums of expression, respectively, trademarks are linked inseparably to goodwill. A trademark has no existence apart from the goodwill of the business it represents. A company's trademark may serve as such a powerful symbol of goodwill that it constitutes one of a company's most valuable assets.

If customers have learned to recognize a particular trademark as indicating the products of a familiar source and/or products of a particular quality, they may be induced to buy a product simply because they find it bearing a familiar trademark. This is true because a trademark not only serves the function of distinguishing the goods or services of a particular source, but also provides an assurance of quality consistency.

13-8   Eligible Subject Matter.   A wide variety of words, names, symbols, article configurations, and other devices, as well as combinations thereof, can serve as trademarks. To serve as a trademark, however, the word, name, symbol, article configuration, or other device must be distinct enough to be protectable in regard to the goods or services with which it is used. There must not be a likelihood that the mark will cause confusion with respect to similar marks used by others for identical or similar goods or services.

A series of letters, numerals, symbols, or various combinations thereof are often used as trademarks. Slogans and pictorial representations may serve as trademarks. Geometric shapes, such as that of a building, can serve a trademark function.

Section 1052 of Title 15 of the United States Code prohibits registration of trademarks that consist of or comprise the following:

1.   Immoral, deceptive or scandalous matter
2.   Matter which may disparage or falsely suggest a connection with, or bring into contempt or dispute, persons, living or dead, institutions, beliefs, or national symbols
3.   The flag or coat of arms or other insignia of the United States, or of any State or municipality, or of any foreign nation, or any simulation thereof

4. A name, portrait, or signature identifying a particular living individual except by his written consent, or

5. The name, signature, or portrait of a deceased President of the United States during the life of his widow, if any, except by the written consent of the widow.

13-9 The Essential Element: Use.   While federal and state governments provide procedures for the registration of trademark rights, these rights themselves are created by *using* a trademark and not through a registration procedure. Trademark rights will continue to exist and be protectable so long as a trademark continues to be used. Use is the key to establishing and maintaining rights in a trademark.

CHAPTER FOURTEEN

Selection and Proper Use of Trademarks

Failure to select a suitably distinctive trademark will handicap efforts to protect, preserve, and establish it as a valuable asset. Failure to use a trademark properly can destroy its value. The two mistakes made most often with respect to trademarks are the failure to select good trademarks from the outset and to properly use trademarks in which valuable rights have been established.

14-1 The Foremost Rule. In selecting a trademark, do not copy the mark of someone else, even partially, even unintentionally. Do not use a mark that trades on the good will of a mark someone else has worked to make known.

It has been held that a newcomer to a product field has a legal duty to select a mark wholly dissimilar to trademarks already being used in the field. Accordingly, it is highly desirable that a trademark search be conducted to ascertain the availability of a mark for adoption and that an opinion be obtained with regard to its registrability. If there is a likelihood that the public may be confused or deceived by a mark one intends to adopt, the owner may be subject to an action for trademark infringement.

By selecting a mark that is sufficiently distinctive to clearly avoid any likelihood of confusion with the marks of others, the owner will be able to effectively enforce his right in court to prevent others from infringing his mark, and he will be able to register his trademark rights. Once a mark has been approved for adoption and has been put into use, consideration should be given to moving forward promptly with steps to register it.

14-2 Protection Scope Depends on Character of Mark. The scope of protection afforded to any particular trademark depends in large measure on the character of the mark itself.

Coined Marks.   A unique, newly coined mark, unknown prior to its adoption and denoting nothing about the goods on which it is used, is entitled to the broadest scope of protection. Coined marks are inherently distinctive and are preferred because there is a minimal likelihood that anyone will have established trademark rights in such marks. A coined mark will therefore be available for expansion to a wide range of products. It will be protectable and registrable immediately on use. A coined mark will be a strong mark in the sense that it will be given judicial protection of broad scope against infringement. An example of a coined mark is Kodak as applied to cameras.

Arbitrary Marks.   A less desirable type of mark, but one, nonetheless, entitled to relatively broad protection is an arbitrary mark. An *arbitrary mark* is one already in linguistic use, but when applied to a certain product or service neither suggests nor describes its features, ingredients, qualities, or characteristics. An arbitrary mark is less desirable than a coined mark because it is already known in the language and may already be in use by others for certain types of products. While an arbitrary mark may be available for adoption and use with regard to a particular product or service, it may not be possible to expand the use of the mark to other products or services in view of the use others have made of the same mark. So long as the use of an arbitrary mark with a particular product or service does not create a likelihood of confusion, the mark will be registrable. An example of an arbitary mark is Shell as applied to petroleum products.

Suggestive Marks.   A third category of trademarks includes those marks that suggest certain features, qualities, ingredients, characteristics, or functions of the product or service for which the mark is used. A suggestive mark is like an arbitrary mark in that it comprises a word, a symbol, or a picture already in common linguistic use. A suggestive mark differs from an arbitrary mark in that it tends to suggest some desirable attribute of the product or service with which it is associated. A suggestive mark is subject to the same dangers, possible weaknesses, lack of expandability to other products, and registrability characteristics as an arbitrary mark. An example of a suggestive mark is Halo as applied to shampoo.

Descriptive Marks.   A fourth category of marks includes those descriptive of the intended purpose or function of a product or service or of some other characteristic of the product or service. While there is a fine line of distinction between suggestive and descriptive marks, a dramatic difference exists in the legal consequences attendant to the two categories of marks. Descriptive marks are not registrable until they have become distinctive over a significant period of time as the result of trademark use, that is, until they have attained *secondary meaning*. There is nothing wrong with using a descriptive mark so long as one realizes that others can use the same or similar words in a proper description of their products. For a descriptive mark to merit trademark registration, it must be shown that the mark has gained such consumer acceptance and recognition that it denotes only one seller or source, i.e., the mark has attained *secondary meaning*. An example of a mark that has been held to be descriptive is Ruberoid, as applied to roofing materials having the characteristics of rubber.

Unprotectable Terms.   Terms totally unprotectable as trademarks are those that are generic, that is, those that refer to the general type or class of product with which they are used. A danger faced by every trademark owner is that buyers may use one's mark as the generic name for a new product or service; the result is that very valuable trademark rights can be lost. The annals of trademark practice are replete with sad tales of such fanciful marks as "Aspirin," "Cellophane," and "Escalator" having been unintentionally relinquished by permitting them to become generic, whereby they have been lost forever as trademarks.

14-3   Avoiding Abandonment.   One must continue to use a trademark properly, or it will be deemed to have been abandoned, thereby opening rights in the mark to the entire world. Once a mark has been abandoned, it may be adopted and used by another entity, who in doing so gains rights himself against the entire world. While an intention to abandon a mark is a prerequisite to its being held to be legally abandoned by nonuse, a period of nonuse of the mark may constitute sufficient evidence from which an intention to abandon may be inferred.

If a trademark owner fails to enforce his rights against infringers, this too may amount to abandonment, for the trademark owner's symbol of origin is lost when others make use of a similar mark. Under the Lanham Act, a mark is deemed to have been abandoned when its use has been discontinued with intent not to resume. Nonuse for two consecutive years raises a presumption of abandonment.

14-4   Selecting a Good Trademark.   In selecting a trademark, a patent attorney would advise the use of nothing other than a coined mark because this type of mark affords the broadest scope of protection and tends to encounter the least difficulty in registration and enforcement. If a coined mark is unacceptable to the client, the next preferred choice is an arbitrary mark.

Suggestive and descriptive marks tend to be preferred by advertising people because these marks are thought to enhance initial product salability. In the long run, however, the many problems that often result from the selection of either a suggestive or a descriptive mark may outweigh any initial advantage such a mark may offer. Descriptive marks are difficult to register and are not entitled to broad protection. Suggestive marks run the risk of being held to be descriptive when efforts are made to register and enforce these marks.

In selecting a trademark, terms that are misdescriptive and laudatory should be avoided. Terms falsely describing the character of goods or a company's business cannot be registered. Laudatory terms indicating the superiority of a product usually make poor trademarks not only because they tend to be descriptive, but also because they are often in use by other companies for a wide variety of products and are therefore entitled to receive only extremely narrow protection, if any.

14-5   Proper Trademark Use.   Proper use of trademarks is absolutely essential to maintaining trademark rights. In the event a trademark is misused by its owner or others and becomes a generic name for a particular type or class of product, the owner will lose his rights in the mark. It is therefore important that a trademark owner understand the rules of proper trademark use so that he will not lose his trademarks by misusing them.

A mistake many trademark owners make is to think of a trademark as a name of a product. Some manufacturers and advertising people select trademarks by deciding on a name for a particular product. Once this has been done, the product is then referred to by its selected name. This is frightfully wrong.

If one has selected as a trademark the coined word Dubicary, it is wrong to refer to products on which the mark is used as Dubicarys. If the product on which the trademark Dubicary is used is a "whamwhat," then there are Dubicary brand "whamwhats;" but there is no such thing as a Dubicary.

In other words, the primary and most important rule of proper trademark usage is that a trademark must *never* be used as a noun. It must *always* be used as a brand name for a particular type of product. The only truly proper way a trademark can be used is as an adjective preceding and modifying a noun. Such nouns as "system," "device," "unit," and the like can be inserted after a trademark to give the mark a noun to modify should there be no better generic term to more accurately describe the product or service. This primary rule of proper trademark usage should not be violated in advertising, in correspondence, or anywhere else one's trademarks are used. Trademark owners must guard against the very natural tendency to refer to a particular product by using a trademark in a noun sense. Trademarks must be recognized as brand names and not as product names.

Since a trademark is not a noun, it must not be used in a plural or possessive sense. Similarly, a trademark is not a verb and must not be used as such. To maintain its distinctiveness the mark should never be abbreviated or be altered by the addition of prefixes or suffixes. Any corruption or change in the form of a mark dilutes its distinctiveness and implies that it is just another word.

Once the exact form of a trademark has been selected and the mark has been used in commerce to establish rights in the mark, the mark should always be used in that exact format. Once a mark has been registered, it should always be used in the exact form in which it has been registered. If a selected or registered form of a mark includes a hyphen or other distinguishing feature, the mark should always be used with this feature.

If the selected or registered form of a mark does not include a logo, design, or other stylized format, then the mark should be distinguished in some other way so it stands out from the text in which it appears. A preferred way of complying with this rule, particularly in advertising, is for the mark to appear in all capital letters with the balance of the text in lowercase letters. In other general writing such as periodicals and newspapers, the accepted form is an initial capital letter; the rest of the description should be in lowercase letters.

Until such time as a trademark has been registered, it is desirable to use the symbol ™ with the mark as an indication of the owner's established rights in the mark. The registration symbol ® should be used in conjunction with the marks that have been registered in the United States Patent and Trademark Office. It is not permissible to use the registration symbol ® in conjunction with marks that have been registered only on a statewide basis. When a registration symbol is used regularly with one's federally registered trademark, one can recover damages or profits for past infringement without having to prove that an infringer had actual notice of the mark's registration.

14-6   Utilizing Trademark Rights to Prevent the Marketing by Others of Look-Alike Products.   While the patent law is intended to permit a competitor to produce functional equivalents of the unpatented products of a company, the law of unfair competition frowns on a competitor who seeks to copy every last feature of the appearance of a company's major products, and then sells the usually foreign-made look-alikes as being the equivalent of the more expensive American-made originals. There was a time when business ethics and etiquette kept these sorts of practices from occurring, but that time seems to have passed. What then can a company properly do to retain customers it has worked for years to satisfy by providing high quality products at reasonable costs?

One approach is to obtain utility patent protection on a timely basis on novel functional features of products as the products are developed. In some instances the 17 years of protection afforded by a utility patent give the protection one needs over a period of time that is sufficient to develop and market an improved product that is also protected by patent coverage.

Another approach is to obtain design patent protection on a timely basis on the ornamental appearances of products as the products are developed. In some instances the 14 years of protection afforded by a design patent serve the need one has for coverage during a time while an improved, more attractive product is being developed which will also be protected by design patent coverage.

In other instances, however, a product is developed which, for totally arbitrary, fanciful, and nonfunctional reasons, includes a number of distinctive features that set this product apart in appearance from products of the competition. Where fanciful features of this sort are included in a product that succeeds in achieving good commercial success, the appearance of the product can come to take on what is called "secondary meaning" whereby, when customers see a product that incorporates these fanciful features, they assume that the product originates with the same source as do other products that incorporate the same fanciful features. Stated in another way, the fanciful features have come to serve the function of a trademark, and the mark can be registered.

In order for trademark rights in a product configuration to form a proper basis for halting competitor marketing of counterfeit look-alike products, it is usually necessary to establish to the satisfaction of the court that the trademark features in question:

1. Are not dictated by functional considerations but rather are fanciful in character

2. Have acquired secondary meaning in the minds of the purchasers

3. Present a likelihood of confusion if incorporated in a competitor's product, and

4. Comprise only one of a number of alternative product configurations, the others of which can be used by competitors to compete effectively in the marketplace.

If trademark rights can be established in the configuration of a product, unlike design or utility patent rights which expire at the end of a 14 or 17 year period, trademark rights can be maintained, enforced, registered and registrations renewed *ad infinitum*. Thus, in view of the endless protection that can result if a product configuration which incorporates fanciful features is put into use and its use maintained to the exclusion of others, it behooves manufacturers to consider incorporating some truly fanciful features in the configurations of their products, and to treat those features as constituting trademarks.

14-7 Markings in Compliance with Federal Law. Trademarks are not the only markings that should be applied to products and/or to packages containing products. There are a variety of federal laws that require various forms of labels and markings for consumer protection and to attest to compliance with federal inspection requirements.

It can be distressing midway through the prosecution of a trademark application to receive an inquiry from the Patent and Trademark Office regarding whether the applicant has complied with labeling requirements of such federal laws as the Meat Inspection Act, the Poultry Products Inspection Act, the Federal Alcohol Administration Act, the Federal Seed Act, the Federal Food, Drug and Cosmetic Act, and others. In this regard, where foodstuffs, drugs, cosmetics, and other products to which federal labeling laws apply are the goods with respect to which a mark is to be registered, it is desirable to deal with the marking requirements of federal law at the time a trademark application is filed by assuring that such trademark usage specimens as are filed with the application include markings that establish compliance with appropriate federal labeling laws.

Other federal labeling laws that require careful compliance are the various Tariff Acts, which require the use of appropriately conspicuous markings to indicate the country of origin of foreign-made products. If your competitor is having look-alike products made abroad and is either importing them with no proper foreign-origin markings, or is removing those markings after the products have cleared United States Customs, the district director of United States Customs in your area will lend a receptive ear to any concerns you may have about possible noncomplying activities of your competitors. Often Customs inspectors are able to intercept incoming shipments of competing products, check them for proper markings, and follow the products through to their final sales point to make certain that proper foreign-origin labels are kept intact. In some instances, personnel of the Federal Trade Commission will also assist in following through to assure that foreign-origin labels are kept in place.

The problems of counterfeit products and improperly marked foreign-origin look-alikes are becoming of increasing importance. A host of new measures to deal with these concerns is in the offing.

14-8 Prepublication Review and Maintaining Specimen Files. Before labels, displays, advertising material, container markings, and the like are approved for printing, they should be reviewed to assure that they conform with the rules of proper trademark use. Once printed materials have been published bearing one's trademarks, samples of these materials should be preserved with care.

It is desirable that a company maintain a separate file for each of its trademarks and that copies of its advertising and other specimens showing use of its marks be inserted in these files. Specimens are often needed to document the fact that one's marks are in use as well as the extent to which the marks have been used. During the pendency of an application to register a trademark, it is not unusual for the examiner handling a trademark application to request that advertising material be supplied describing the goods or services with which the mark is associated or that other specimens be presented showing how the trademark is used. Specimens showing trademark use are also needed to accompany an affidavit of continued use, which must be filed in the Patent and Trademark Office between the fifth and sixth years after a trademark registration issues, if the registration is to be maintained in force.

CHAPTER FIFTEEN

Trademark Registration

Outlined in this chapter are procedures to follow to register trademarks and maintain and renew existing registrations. As is pointed
out, because one has obtained a registration does not mark the end of
the efforts required to maintain the registration in force.

15-1 Eligibility for Federal Registration. Trademark rights in a
mark are generated as soon as use of the mark, in a trademark sense,
has begun. Registration of trademark rights cannot be pursued until
use has begun. States registration is available in the state or states
where a mark is used. Federal registration may be obtained once a
mark has been put into use in such commerce as may be lawfully reg-
ulated by Congress, usually interstate commerce.

Federal registration of a trademark is generally preferred to state
registration. It may be desirable to obtain a state registration and
maintain it in force until such time as use of the mark has expanded to
include interstate commerce. State registrations occasionally are also
pursued when particularly important marks are involved and the
trademark owners desire to do everything possible to maximize the
extent of their trademark protection.

In our country, registration of a mark cannot be sought or obtained
until the mark has actually been used in a trademark sense in conjunction with the sale of goods or services. Similarly, there is no way
to reserve a trademark for later use. American procedure is unlike
that of some foreign nations where registrations may be obtained before marks have been used.

While an application to register a trademark can be filed many
years after the mark was first put into use, advantages can stem from

filing promptly after a mark has been put into use. The earlier an application is filed, the earlier it can be registered and eventually rendered incontestable through the approval of an affidavit filed with the Patent and Trademark Office to document five years of continuous and exclusive use of a registered mark. Moreover, if one's application to register is put on file *before* a third party first uses the same mark, the third party will have no standing to oppose the issuance of a registration because the third party legally cannot be damaged by the issuance of a registration.

15-2 Categories of Federal Registration. The Lanham Act establishes five categories under which marks may be registered:

1. The Principal Register, trademarks section
2. The Principal Register, service marks section
3. The Principal Register, collective marks section
4. The Principal Register, certification marks section
5. The Supplemental Register.

The Principal Register is for marks that unquestionably serve to distinguish goods or services in interstate commerce. The Supplemental Register is for marks that, for a reason such as descriptiveness, are not registrable on the Principal Register until they acquire secondary meaning.

Registration of a mark on the Principal Register provides several procedural and substantive advantages over reliance on common law rights. Principal Register registration provides constructive notice to the public of the registrant's claim to rights in the mark. Constructive notice prevents a latecomer from claiming that he had no notice of the existing registration and therefore adopted his mark in good faith.

A Principal Register registration may be used as a basis to stop importation of goods bearing an infringing trademark. Principal Register registration also gives access to the federal courts without regard to such other requirements as diversity of citizenship or an adequate amount in controversy, both of which could constitute significant hurdles to the enforcement of trademark rights in the absence of a federal registration.

Principal Register registration affords several presumptions, including that (1) the registrant owns the mark, (2) the mark has been in continuous use dating back to the filing date of the application, (3) the mark is not confusingly similar to other registered marks, (4) the mark has acquired secondary meaning, and (5) the mark has been used in interstate commerce before registration.

While Supplemental Register registration provides access to the federal courts in the same manner as a Principal Register registration, it neither serves as constructive notice nor provides any of the presumptions associated with Principal Register registration. Before a mark can be registered on the Supplemental Register, it must have been in use for the one year period that precedes the filing of an application. This one year requirement can be waived by the Commissioner of Patents and Trademarks if the applicant shows that he requires a domestic registration to be able to obtain foreign protection of his mark.

That a mark is registered on the Supplemental Register does not preclude its later being registered on the Principal Register if the mark has become eligible for Principal Register registration. Once an applicant has presented satisfactory evidence of the fact that he has made exclusive and continuous use of a mark in commerce for the five year period preceding the date on which an application is filed for Principal Register registration, the mark will be presumed to have become distinctive. Such a presumption of distinctiveness will overcome any objection to the registration of the mark as being "merely descriptive."

15-3 State Registration. State registration will usually have little legal significance other than to serve as proof that on a certain date the registrant has filed an application stating that he has been using a certain mark. Some states do give trademark registration a greater effect by holding that a registration provides a presumption of ownership. In most states, however, state trademark registration is akin to Supplemental Register registration in that it does not provide much in the way of substantive rights.

One benefit a state registration may provide is that it may tend to deter others from adopting one's mark if, for example, the state registration is found during a search conducted by another entity before selecting a new trademark for adoption.

The majority of state trademark registrations last for a period of 10 years and are renewable at the end of that period. A few states provide longer terms, some being perpetual.

15-4 Registration Procedure. Filing an application to register a trademark is ordinarily not complex. The application must present certain basic information, including the name and address of the applicant, and must include a description of the goods or services with which the mark is used. The class or classes of goods or services must be stated, as must certain information regarding the date of first use of the mark.

A federal trademark registration application must state the date of first use of the mark anywhere, as well as the date of its first use in interstate commerce, and must be accompanied by five specimens showing the mark as it is actually used, together with a drawing of the mark. A filing fee, the magnitude of which depends on the number of classes into which the named goods or services fall, must be submitted concurrently with the application. Additionally, the application must include a declaration or oath as is prescribed by law. Federal trademark applications cannot be signed by an applicant's attorney, but must be signed by the applicant himself. In the case of a corporation, the application must be signed by an officer of the corporation.

As of this writing the fee charged by the Office for filing a trademark application stands at $175. If the goods for which registration is sought fall in more than one Office classification, an additional fee of $175 is charge for each additional class.

15-5 Patent and Trademark Office Procedure. Once an executed application has been received by the Patent and Trademark Office, it is assigned a filing date and serial number. The application is inspected initially to make certain it is formally sufficient. The back-log of applications in the Office causes a registrability examination delay. While this delay has traditionally extended for a period of several months, the Office is rapidly diminishing it. Once the application reaches the attention of the examiner to whom it has been assigned, he conducts a search of the records of the Patent and Trademark Office to determine the registrability of the mark. The examiner informs the applicant of his findings in a communication called an Office Action.

In some instances, the first Office Action may take the form of a Notice of Publication informing the applicant that the application has been accepted and will be published in the *Official Gazette* on a designated date. As is more often the case, however, the examiner will have some objection or further question and will issue an objection and/or a rejection. In these instances, the applicant is presently being given six months to reply by amending his application, requesting reconsideration, or taking such other action as the applicant believes will assist in forwarding prosecution of the case. As efforts to "compact" the prosecution time of trademark applications are implemented by the Office, the traditional six months response time may be reduced significantly.

In responding to an Office Action, technical objections are usually relatively easy to overcome. Such objections ordinarily take the form of objections to the wording of the application, particularly to the wording of the description of goods or services. If the examiner has rejected the application, the applicant will normally reply by filing an amendment that makes such changes in the application as are needed to overcome the objections made by the examiner and/or by filing a response that sets forth a rebuttal.

While a personal interview with the examiner is seldom necessary to successfully prosecute a trademark application, an interview in person or by telephone may be of assistance in supplementing the arguments being made or in obtaining a better understanding of the position taken by the examiner.

Once an application has been accepted for publication, it is pub-

lished in the Trademarks Section of the *Official Gazette*. Publication
of a trademark subjects it to the possibility of opposition by parties
who believe they may be damaged by the issuance of a registration.
Parties who believe they might be damaged have 30 days from the
date of publication to oppose the registration.

In the event that no opposition is instituted, the ultimate registration certificate usually does not issue for two to four months after the
date of publication. If an opposition is instituted, jurisdiction of this
activity is vested in the Trademark Trial and Appeal Board, where a
proceeding similar to a federal court lawsuit takes place to determine
whether a registration will be issued.

The ultimate issue to be resolved in an opposition proceeding is
whether the applicant has a sufficient exclusive right to use the mark
to justify registration. Likelihood of confusion, prior use as a trade
name, ownership of a prior registration, and a host of other grounds
may be advanced as grounds for sustaining an opposition.

15-6   Maintaining a Registration in Force.   Unless a Section 8 Affidavit is filed between the fifth and sixth anniversaries of the date of
issuance of a federal trademark registration, the registration is automatically cancelled on the sixth anniversary. The purpose of requiring the filing of a Section 8 Affidavit is to remove from the Register
those marks no longer in use. A Section 8 Affidavit must include a
statement that the mark is still in use; it must specify the naure of such
use and include a specimen, facsimile, or other evidence showing the
mark as currently used. Alternatively, the affidavit must present sufficient facts to show that nonuse is a result of special circumstances
which excuse nonuse, and that nonuse is not due to any intention to
abandon the mark.

Anytime within one year after the expiration of the five-year period of continuous use of a registered trademark, a Section 15 Affidavit
may be filed to render a Principal Register registration incontestable.
A registration that has been rendered incontestible can be attacked
only on a limited number of bases such as fraudulent procurement,

abandonment of the mark, or misuse. Attaining the status of incontestability clearly buttresses the legal status of the trademark.

Whenever possible, it is desirable to file a Section 15 Affidavit concurrently with the filing of a Section 8 Affidavit. If it is anticipated that these two testimonials will be filed concurrently, they can be combined in the form of a single affidavit.

Federal trademark registrations issuing under the Lanham Act remain in force for a term of 20 years and may be renewed indefinitely for additional 20 year periods. Renewal is effected by filing an application that includes a suitable affidavit or declaration, a specimen showing current use of the mark, and the required filing fee. Such an application must be filed within the six month period preceding a 20 year expiration date, or it can be filed within three months after the expiration date.

Under suitable circumstances, existing registrations may be cancelled through a cancellation proceeding. Cancellation can be sought by one who believes he will be damaged by the continuing existence of the registration. A cancellation proceeding is initiated by filing a petition to cancel and is conducted much like an opposition proceeding.

CHAPTER SIXTEEN

Assigning, Licensing, and Enforcing Trademark Rights

This chapter touches briefly on two significant bodies of law, the first relating to the sale and licensing of trademarks, the second to trademark infringement.

16-1 Trademark Assignments. An *assignment* is an outright sale of all rights in the mark. Since trademarks are regarded as property, they can be bought and sold.

A pitfall to avoid in the purchase and sale of a trademark has to do with the goodwill of the business associated with the mark. A trademark has no independent significance apart from the goodwill it symbolizes. Accordingly, a trademark cannot be purchased or sold apart from the goodwill of the business it symbolizes. If one obtains a trademark through a sale without having concurrently received the attendant goodwill, the continuity of the thing symbolized by the mark is broken and the sale is unquestionably deficient.

An assignment of common law rights in a trademark does not need to be in writing to be effective. Assignments of federal trademark applications and registrations, however, must take the form of duly executed documents. While federal recordation of an assignment is not mandatory, it is advisable. Recordation of an assignment promptly following its execution will maximize one's protection.

16-2 Trademark Licensing. Trademarks may be licensed by their owners. When a third party is licensed to use a trademark, the license agreement must include provisions spelling out reasonable steps to prevent misuses of the licensed trademark by the licensee so the public is not deceived. Unless appropriate quality control measures are enforced by the licensor, the license agreement may be deemed to be a "naked" or "bare" license, that is, a license that has been held to constitute a fraud on the public. Uncontrolled or naked licensing may result in a trademark's ceasing to function as a symbol of quality. Uncontrolled licensing can result in such a loss of significance of the trademark that its federal registration may qualify for cancellation.

The degree of quality control that must be exercised by the licensor of a trademark over his licensee is not precisely clear in case law interpreting this requirement. The question is not whether the licensor *has* the right to control the quality of the products or services of the licensee, but whether, in fact, the licensor *exercises* the required degree of control.

Peculiar problems are encounterd in many foreign countries where efforts are undertaken to establish international trademark licensing programs. In countries that follow British law, for example, there is a requirement that a licensee be approved as a *registered user* and that some memorial of his trademark license agreement be recorded to insure its validity. In many Latin American countries, government approval must be obtained for trademark licenses, and in some instances, such licenses are prohibited. In short, licensing trademarks abroad varies considerably from country to country and often requires the assistance of someone familiar with the various and changing provisions of trademark laws of the countries involved.

16-3 Trademark Infringement. The most accepted test for trademark infringement is that of *likelihood of confusion*. It is not necessary for an infringer to have any wrongful intent to be liable for trademark infringement. Liability exists when the use one makes of a mark may cause a likelihood of confusion with the trademark rights established earlier by another entity. The question of whether likelihood of confusion is an issue of law or an issue of fact has given rise to conflicting decisions in the Circuit Courts of Appeal. The newly established Court of Appeals for the Federal Circuit has held that likelihood of confusion is a conclusion of law.

In a trademark infringement action, injunctive relief may be obtained before the occurrence of actual injury if the trademark owner can prove the existence of a likelihood of confusion and hence a likelihood of injury. Monetary recovery for trademark infringement may be had in several forms, including an award measured by the infringer's profits, an award measured by actual damages caused by the infringement, an award measured by the loss of profits caused by the infringement, an award of punitive damages intended to punish the infringer, and an award of reasonable attorney's fees incurred in prosecuting trademark infringement action. Punitive damages are awarded only when the infringer's conduct has been outrageous. Recovery of attorney's fees is permitted only in very exceptional situations.

REFERENCES

Diamond, Sidney A., *Trademark Problems and How to Avoid Them*, Crain, Chicago, 1973, 1981.

Gilson, Jerome, *Trademark Protection and Practice*, Matthew Bender, New York, 1974.

McCarthy, J. Thomas, *Trademarks and Unfair Competition*, Lawyers Co-Operative Publishing, Rochester, New York, 1973.

Trademark Manual of Examining Procedure, Government Printing Office, 1st Ed., Jan. 1974, latest rev. December, 1982.

Vandenburg, Edward C., III, *Trademark Law and Procedure*, 2nd ed., Bobbs-Merrill, New York, 1968.

PART FOUR

OTHER FORMS OF INTELLECTUAL PROPERTY

CHAPTER SEVENTEEN
Design Patents

A design patent is one medium for obtaining protection of nonfunctional features of useful objects. A design patent may be obtained on a new, original, ornamental, and nonobvious design embodied in or on an article of manufacture.

17-1 The Requirement of Ornamentality. To be ornamental, a design must present a pleasing aesthetic appearance. It must appear to the eye as a thing of beauty. The design must not be dictated solely by functional considerations. If the article of manufacture has utilitarian or functional features, these must not predominate in determining the design. In other words, a design need not meet the requirement of utility, which must be met by a utility patent, and indeed is not patentable if its form is dictated entirely by considerations of functionality.

17-2 Novelty and Nonobviousness Requirements. To be patentable, a design must meet the requirements of novelty and nonobviousness. The same novelty requirements discussed in conjunction with utility patent applications must be met by design inventions. A design will not satisfy these novelty requirements if it is fully anticipated by a prior design, even though the prior design relates to an article of manufacture having a different use from the article to which the design in question is applied.

The requirement of nonobviousness is a difficult one to apply to designs. The assessment of nonobviousness of a design must, of necessity, be entirely subjective. A design is not patentable if its only points of novelty or nonobviousness are dictated by functional considerations alone.

17-3   Embodiment in an Article of Manufacture.   A design must be embodied in an article of manufacture to be patentable. A patentable design is inseparable from the object on which it appears. A patentable design cannot exist alone merely as a scheme of surface ornamentation. To be patentable, a design must be a definite, preconceived thing capable of being reproduced. A patentable design may relate to the configuration or shape of an article of manufacture, to its surface ornamentation, or to a combination of these things.

17-4   Application Content.   A design patent application is much less complex than a utility patent application. With a utility patent application the written description is ordinarily deemed to be of greater importance than the drawings; the situation is exactly reversed in the case of a design patent application.

The principal disclosure in a design case is provided by the drawings. The Patent and Trademark Office is therefore particularly fastidious about the character of the drawings submitted with a design patent application. The drawings must contain a sufficient number of views to provide a complete disclosure of the entire appearance of the article. Nothing regarding the shape, configuration, and surface ornamentation of the article may be left to conjecture. If the drawings of a design application fail to disclose the entire appearance of an article, the design patent application will be deemed to be incomplete.

While it is possible to use dotted or broken lines in a design patent drawing to indicate related environmental structures that do not form a part of the design, the specification of the design patent application must make it clear that the structure shown in broken lines is not part of the design.

A design patent application includes only a single claim. One of the few requirements with regard to the character of a design patent claim is that it must designate the particular article of manufacture on which design patent protection is sought. The scope of claim coverage may be enhanced by including in the claim the words "or similar article."

It is usually unnecessary for a design patent application to include any description of the claimed design other than a brief description of the drawing figures. If there is a description of the design, it should be of the appearance of the article. In the event an appropriate title cannot adequately designate the nature and use of the article of manufacture, some further description of the article will be permitted.

17-5   Patent and Trademark Office Procedure.   Design patent applications are handled by the Patent and Trademark Office in substantially the same manner described in Chapter 6, which relates to utility patents. Since a design patent application includes only a single claim, prosecution of a design case is ordinarily less involved than is the prosecution of a utility case.

Once a design patent issues, the protection it provides has a term of 14 years. In earlier years it was possible for an applicant to select a term of $3\frac{1}{2}$, 7, or 14 years.

17-6   Infringement and Enforcement.   The conventional infringement recoveries discussed in Chapter 7 relating to utility patent infringement are available to the design patent owner. Additionally, Section 289 of Title 35 of the United States Code provides a special remedy for infringement of a design patent. This special remedy permits a design patent owner to recover the total extent of an infringer's profits, but not less than $250.

17-7   Design Patent and Copyright Law Overlap.   There is a degree of overlap between design patent law and copyright law. Copyright protection for the design of a useful object is obtainable to the extent that the design incorporates pictorial, graphic, or sculptural features that can be identified separately from, and are capable of existing independently of, the utilitarian aspects of the article. If a design is not capable of existing independently from the article, copyright protection is not available. A great many designs are patentable, but are not copyrightable, because these designs do not meet the copyright requirement of separate identification and independent existence.

Examples of designs commonly copyrighted include such works of art as jewelry, glassware, tapestries, paintings, drawings, and sculptures. Copyright registration of these works offers advantages over design patent protection because of the much longer term afforded to copyright registrations. Moreover, the copyright laws do not require that the works of art be novel or inventive, although they must be original with the artist or author who claims copyright. Design patent protection has the advantage over copyright protection of covering infringing articles regardless of whether they were produced through "copying" or by independent efforts.

The Copyright Office will not permit a copyright registration to issue on a design that has been patented, or on drawings or photographs used in an issued patent. While it has been held that a design patent can be obtained on a design that has already been made the subject of a copyright registration, there are those who would argue that one should be required to elect between either a copyright or a design patent approach in pursuing protection.

17-8   Design Patent and Trademark Law Overlap.   Trademark rights may be generated in the configuration of an article if that configuration has come to acquire a secondary meaning through use. Secondary meaning occurs when a configuration, such as the shape of a bottle in which a soft drink or perfume is sold, has come to be associated with a particular source of supply of the soft drink or perfume.

If one is to secure the right to exclude others from using a container design, it may be desirable during the early years of use of the design to pursue design patent protection. In later years, if the configuration of the container has genuinely taken on secondary meaning because of its extensive use, it should be possible to obtain trademark registration of the container configuration. If one can obtain trademark registration under these circumstances, one can secure, on an essentially permanent basis, his rights in the container configuration.

Some court decisions criticize the possibility of obtaining trademark registration on the configuration of an article that has also been covered by a design patent. In making this criticism, the argument is advanced that a trademark should not be permitted to effectively extend the scope of protection afforded by a design patent. Despite this criticism, however, it is believed that the trend of the law will continue to permit trademark protection to be used to secure one's rights in a design (regardless of whether it has been patented) in circumstances where the design has genuinely taken on secondary meaning.

A trademark-worthy design need not be entirely nonutilitarian. Indeed, if a design has come to serve the function of a trademark, it would constitute a fraud on the public to permit others to use the design in such a manner as might cause a likelihood of confusion.

CHAPTER EIGHTEEN

Plant Protection

The practice of providing protection on plant varieties is relatively new to our country. Congress first provided for this possibility in 1930. Two avenues of protection are available, namely, through the issuance of a plant patent by the Patent and Trademark Office or a certificate of plant variety protection from the Department of Agriculture.

Protecting compositions of matter that are not products of nature, and the relatively broad subject of biotechnology in general are treated in Chapter 22.

18-1 Plant Patents. A plant patent may be obtained by a person who invents or discovers, and who also asexually reproduces a distinct and new variety of plant, other than a tuber-propagated plant or a plant found in an uncultivated state. A person who identified the characteristics of a new variety of plant and causes it to be asexually reproduced may obtain a plant patent even though he did not cultivate the new variety. To be patentable, a new variety of plant must meet the requirement of nonobviousness.

A plant patent confers the right to exclude others from asexually reproducing the plant or from selling or using a patented plant that has been asexually reproduced. One does not infringe a plant patent by sexually reproducing the plant, that is, by reproduction through the use of seeds. Reproduction must take place asexually, such as by the rooting of cuttings, layering, budding, grafting, inarching, and the like. Asexual reproduction assures that the exact characteristics of a plant are maintained. Plants amenable to plant patent protection include shrubs, vines, roses, and various types of fruit and nut trees.

A plant patent application must include drawings that disclose all the distinctive plant characteristics capable of visual representation. The application must describe the plant as fully as possible. A plant patent has a term of 17 years.

18-2   Certificates of Plant Variety Protection.   Protection of sexually reproduced plants may be obtained under the provisions of the Plant Variety Protection Act of 1970, which is administered by the Department of Agriculture.

One who holds a certificate of plant variety protection is given the exclusive right to sell, reproduce, import, export, and otherwise use the novel plant variety or its seed. A certificate of plant variety protection had a term of 17 years until 1980, when the term was changed to 18 years.

Two provisions of the Plant Protection Act are of interest, for they have no counterpart in the patent law. One is the right given to the Secretary of Agriculture to shorten the term of protection "by the amount of delay in prosecution of the application" that is attributable to the applicant if a certificate has not issued within three years from the filing date. The other is that the term of protection expires if the applicant fails to replenish the seed of his variety in a public depository.

18-3   Utility Patent Protection.   "Manufactures" and "compositions of matter" that are man-made and do not occur in nature may be protected by a utility patent, assuming the tests of patentability discussed in Chapter 4 are also met. Chapter 22 treats these subjects.

CHAPTER NINETEEN

Copyrights

The Copyright Revision Act of 1976 became effective January 1, 1978, significantly modernizing copyright practice. This new law superseded and strengthened the outdated Copyright Act of 1909. The old law had undergone only minor changes during its long existence and was not well adapted to deal with the technological changes that have taken place since 1909.

Under the new law, every work of original authorship is born with an inherent copyright. This reduces the problem of copyright protection to one of preserving what came naturally, by using proper copyright notices and following other requirements of the law.

A specific discussion of applications of the copyright law to the protection of computer technology is presented in Chapter 21.

19-1 Comparison to Patents. While patents and copyrights are two types of intellectual property protections that have had parallel development, and while both are supported by the same sentence appearing in Article I, Section 8 of the Constitution, patents and copyrights are not the same. These two types of protections are controlled by different statutory provisions, administered by different agencies of government, and cover different classes of subject matter.

Patent protection essentially extends to new works of the industrial artist, whose inventions relate to the useful arts. Copyright protection essentially extends to works of the fine artist, whose creations are expressed in such media as music, literature, and the aesthetic arts.

Copyright protection does not extend to mere ideas or thoughts. Just as ideas, per se, may not be patented, neither may they be copyrighted. However, when an idea or thought is embodied in a particular form of expression, that form of expression may be entitled to copyright protection.

A principal difference in the respective statutes relating to patents and copyrights is the manner in which patents and copyrights are infringed. While a patent is infringed through the unauthorized making, using, or selling of a claimed invention regardless of whether the infringement was the result of copying, a copyright can only be infringed by someone who actually copies that which is copyrighted. Hence, if a person operates entirely independently and originates material that happens to be covered by a copyright, this person's activities do not amount to copyright infringement.

In proving copyright infringement, one can rarely establish copying by direct evidence. Witnesses who saw the copying take place are seldom available to prove the case. Accordingly, the courts acknowledge an inference of copying when evidence exists that the defendant has had access to the copyrighted work and substantial similarity occurs between the copyrighted work and the allegedly infringing copy.

A copyright owner holds a number of rights, including the right to print, reprint, copy, sell, and distribute the copyrighted work and copies thereof; the right to prepare derivative works based on the copyrighted work; and the right to sell or license this property. The new law acknowledges that these rights can be divided and dealt with independently. Any rights not expressly transferred to another are presumed by the new law to be retained by the author.

19-2 Authorship, Originality, and Fixation Requirements. Under the new law, the principal requirements for pursuing copyright protection are authorship, originality, and fixation in a tangible form. However, the creator or originator of a work may *not* be considered to be its owner or "author." If the originator of the work prepared the work as an activity that was within the scope of his employment, the employer is considered to be the author or rightful owner of the copyright rights in the work under what is called the *work for hire* doctrine. Even a volunteer worker who was paid nothing for his effort may be considered an employee for purposes of determining copyright ownership, especially when the entity for which the volunteer was working had the right to direct and supervise the manner in which the originator performed his work.

Stated in another way, in order for a work to be the property of the entity who authorized its creation by another, the creator must either create the work within the scope of his employment, or the work must be prepared under written agreement as a work for hire. Unless a creator of a work creates a work within the scope of his employment, a written document signed by the creator of the work will be deemed to have created a "work made for hire." An oral order or commission from a nonemployer to an author will leave copyright rights residing in the author. Only the owner of one of the copyright rights in a work is entitled to file to register a copyright.

The authors of a joint work are co-owners of copyright in the work. A *joint work* is one prepared by two or more authors with the intention that their contributions be merged into inseparable or interdependent parts of a unitary whole.

A work satisfies the requirement of fixation if it assumes a sufficiently permanent or stable form to permit its being perceived, reproduced, or communicated for more than a transitory period in any medium of expression, whether the medium of expression is now known or later developed. One cannot copyright a mere idea regardless how brilliant; rather, what is copyrighted is the expression of the idea which must be *fixed* as by being written, put on tape, or the like. Clearly the 1976 Act was not intended to limit the medium in which the work is fixed either by present technology or by future technological developments.

19-3   What Can Be Copyrighted.   Several broad classes of copyrightable works are listed in the 1976 Act. Even though a particular work does not fit precisely into one of these classes, it may still be copyrightable.

Examples of works that may be copyrighted include books, pamphlets, leaflets, greeting cards, periodicals, lectures prepared for oral delivery, dramatic compositions, musical compositions, maps, paintings, drawings, sculptural works, prints, photographs, pictorial illustrations, motion pictures, cartoons, and sound recordings.

Materials that cannot be copyrighted include standard calendars, height and weight charts, tape measures and rulers, schedules of events taken from common sources, and other works consisting solely of information that is common property and that includes no originality of authorship. Also failing to qualify for copyright protection, unless suitable additional original subject matter is present, are blank forms, account books, score cards, ideas, methods of doing business, titles, names, slogans, and lists of ingredients. While copyright protection extends to pictorial, graphic, and sculptural works, an exception excludes works that are defined as "useful articles," namely articles that have an appearance which is dictated by intrinsic utilitarian function or which is designed to convey information. Thus, industrial products such as automobiles and household appliances cannot be subjects of copyright protection.

19-4 Registration Procedure. An unpublished work, that is, a work that has not been sold, placed on sale, or otherwise made available to the public, may be registered by following this procedure:

1. Reducing the work to some suitable tangible form
2. Depositing with the Copyright Office
   (a) An appropriate application form
   (b) A copy of the work
   (c) The requisite registration fee.

A work about to be published may be registered by this procedure:

1. Providing copies of the work with a suitable copyright notice
2. Publishing the work bearing the notice
3. Depositing with the Copyright Office
   (a) An appropriate application form
   (b) Two copies of the work as published
   (c) The requisite registration fee.

A published work may be registered, if it has been published with the requisite copyright notice, by depositing with the Copyright Office an appropriate application form, two copies of the work as published, and the requisite registration fee. There is no time limit for applying to register one's copyright when a work has been published with the requisite copyright notice. However, registration within five years of publication is required if one is to enjoy the presumption of validity that ordinarily accompanies a copyright registration.

A work published without the requisite copyright notice may only be registered if an application to register is filed within five years of the first publication and if reasonable efforts have been made to add the missing notice to all copies that may have been distributed to the public without a proper copyright notice. The 1976 Act does, however, forgive the omission of notice from a relatively small number of copies, so long as the omission was genuinely unintentional. Registration is effected by depositing with the Copyright Office an appropriate application form, two copies of the work as published, and the requisite registration fee.

It is possible to expedite the handling of a copyright registration. On June 1, 1982, the Copyright Office began charging a special handling fee to expedite the processing of a registration. The fee was set at $120 in addition to the registration fee which, as of this writing, stands at $10.

19-5   Term of Protection.   Under the 1976 Act, the duration of copyright life is extended to include the life of the author, plus 50 years. This extended term of copyright protection applies to works created after January 1, 1978. When a joint work has been prepared by two or more authors, the term of the copyright extends for the life of the last surviving author, plus 50 years. In the case of works made for hire, since the "author" may be a company employing the person who created the work, the author may have a perpetual life. Accordingly, the term of copyright protection extending to all works made for hire is 75 years from the date of first publication, or 100 years from the date of creation, whichever expires first.

Under the 1909 Act, copyrights were effective for a term of 28 years and were renewable on the payment of an additional fee for a second term of 28 years. The 1978 Act provides several rules of transition from the 1909 Act. Works created before January 1, 1978, but not published until after January 1, 1978, are assigned a term of copyright plus 50 years, with the exception that the term of copyright protection for these works shall not expire before December 31, 2002. Other transitional rules include a provision that any copyright which issued under the 1909 Act and which is in its first term as of January 1, 1978, shall endure for a period of 28 years from the date it was originally secured and may then be renewed for a further term of 47 years on application to the Copyright Office. In the case of a copyright perfected under the 1909 Act and in its renewal term as of January 1, 1978, the term is automatically extended to 75 years from the date the copyright was originally secured.

19-6 Notice Requirement. The 1976 Act continues the requirement of the 1909 Act calling for each published work to bear a proper copyright notice. A proper copyright notice normally includes the following three elements.

1. The symbol © or the term "Copyright" or the abbreviation "Copr." (or the symbol ℗ for phonorecords)
2. The year of first publication of the work (this may be omitted in some instances)
3. The name of the owner of the copyright or an abbreviation by which the name can be recognized or a generally known alternative designation of the owner.

The new law relaxes previous rules regarding placement of a copyright notice. Instead of spelling out specific required notice locations, the 1976 Act indicates that notices will be sufficient if they are presented "in such manner and location as to give reasonable notice of the claim of copyright."

19-7 Deposit Requirement. The registration process is separate and apart from the deposit requirement of the copyright law. Indeed, under the new law registration is optional. However, there is a deposit requirement of the law that should not be ignored. When a work is first published bearing a copyright notice, within three months two complete copies should be deposited with the Copyright Office. While failure to comply with this requirement does not jeopardize copyright rights, it may incur monetary penalties.

19-8   Features of the New Copyright Act.   A significant change made by the 1976 Act is the provision of a single national system for the protection of copyrights. Under the old law, rights in unpublished works were not protected by federal statute. Under the 1976 Act all works in tangible form, whether published or not, are exclusively protected by the federal statute.

While the 1909 Act did not federally recognize rights in unpublished, unregistered works, the 1976 Act causes federally recognized rights to exist in an unpublished, unregistered work beginning with that instant in time when the work has been created by reducing it to some tangible form. One may opt to register these rights at any time subsequent to creation of the work. However, one may not enforce a copyright under the 1976 Act until a registration actually has been obtained.

The new law recognizes recording as a method of fixing a work in a tangible form. Accordingly, a work that has been dictated is protected even though it may never be transcribed. Protection is also extended to computer programs, data bases, and cable television systems.

Other significant features of the 1976 Act are its provisions dealing with the doctrine of fair use and its relaxation of previous law which dictated that if a work was published without the required copyright notice, it was forever dedicated to the public. The 1976 Act expands and codifies the common law doctrine of fair use, whereby one's copyright may not be asserted to prevent limited uses of a copyrighted work for such purposes as criticisms, news reporting, scholarship, and research. However, a use is not "fair" where it has the effect of substantially diminishing the potential market for a copyrighted work or its value to the copyright owner.

19-9 Benefits of Registration. While registration is not essential to obtaining copyright protection, several rights and benefits do result from pursuing timely registration. If registration is made within five years of the date of first publication, the issuance of a certificate of registration generates a presumption of validity of the copyright and of the facts stated in the registration certificate. Unless registration is pursued within three months of the first publication of a work, no award of statutory damages or of attorney's fees may be made for any copyright infringement begun after publication of the work and before the effective date of registration of the work. For this reason, it is desirable, in many instances, to move ahead with registration of a copyright within three months of the date of first publication.

The law provides that no award of statutory damages or of attorney's fees may be made for any infringement of a copyright in an unpublished work when the infringement was begun before the date of registration of the unpublished work.

19-10 Assignment of a Copyright. A copyright may be transferred or assigned by a document signed by the copyright owner. If the work has been registered, then assignments, licenses, and other documents affecting the title to the work can be recorded in the Copyright Office. For most effective protection, an assignment of a copyright should be recorded in the Copyright Office within three months of its date of execution. A properly recorded document pertaining to a copyright operates to give constructive notice to the public of its content.

CHAPTER TWENTY

Trade Secrets

Because trade secrets are treated late in this book should not be interpreted as indicating that they are of lesser importance than the various other types of intellectual property. To the contrary, many companies consider trade secrets to be their most valuable assets.

20-1 The Nature of Trade Secrets. It is not unusual, in court decisions dealing with trade secrets, to find an expression of exasperation in attempting to define the term "trade secret." The term has application to such a wide range of business information that a universally acceptable definition to difficult to frame.

The definition most frequently cited originates with the *Restatement of Torts* (1939), which begins:

> A trade secret may consist of any formula, pattern, device or compilation of information used in one's business, which gives him an opportunity to obtain an advantage over competitors who do not know or use it. It may be a formula for a chemical compound, a process of manufacturing, treating or preserving materials, a pattern for a machine or other device, or a list of customers . . . A trade secret is a process or device for continuous use in the operation of the business. Generally it relates to the production of goods, as for example, a machine or formula for an article. It may, however, relate to the sale of goods or to other operations in the business, such as a code for determining discounts, rebates or other concessions in a price list or catalogue, or a list of specialized customers, or a method of bookkeeping or other office management.

A trade secret may constitute any information that is not generally known in a trade. It may consist of a combination of items of information, each of which may be in the public domain, but which have not been assembled in unique combination by others. Knowing which pieces of information to select and how they should be combined to give one an advantage over competitors can, in and of itself, constitute an extremely valuable trade secret. That individual features of an assemblage of information are in the public domain does not destroy the trade secret status of these features unless the exact assemblage of features is known in the trade and the value of the exact assemblage is understood by those in the trade.

20-2 Relationship to Patents. A trade secret does not have to be patentable to merit protection. It does not need to be new, nonobvious, or satisfy any of the other attributes of a patentable invention. Almost by definition, a trade secret will have utility, but the traditional tests of patentability do not have to be satisfied.

One of the few things that cannot constitute the subject matter of one's trade secret is his patented invention. Since the patent laws require a full disclosure of the "best mode" known to a patentee for carrying out his invention at the time he files a patent application and since a patent application must, by law, present a sufficiently full and complete description to enable one skilled in the art to which the invention pertains to practice the invention, it is clear that one cannot claim both patent rights and trade secret rights in the same invention.

As is often the case, however, at the time a patent application is filed, the invention it describes may represent chiefly the product of laboratory experimentation. After the patent application has been filed and once efforts have begun to introduce the results of laboratory experimentation into a production environment, a great deal of additional information may be developed that is important to the proper practice of the invention in a production environment. This newly developed production expertise may take on a value at least equal to, if not greater than, that of the patented subject matter. If this newly developed production expertise is properly guarded as a trade secret, can be used without others learning of its content, constitutes a development others are unlikely to make, and gives one an economic advantage over competitors who do not know of it, then it may be a very valuable trade secret. Under proper contractual conditions, others may be willing to pay handsome royalties for the privilege of being permitted to use the trade secret.

If the subject matter being considered for retention as a trade secret is patentable, the advantages and disadvantages of patenting an invention or maintaining it as a trade secret must be weighed carefully. One advantage of a trade secret is that it will not automatically become dedicated to the public at the end of 17 years as is the case with patents. On the other hand, the competitive advantage provided by a trade secret may evaporate overnight if the secret becomes available to the public or if another reseacher should independently develop the same information. Moreover, if one attempts to maintain patentable subject matter as a trade secret, there is the danger that another may invent it and obtain patent protection of his own. Should this happen, the second inventor will have the right to exact royalties from the first or to compel the first to cease infringement.

When one has the opportunity to patent an invention or maintain it as a trade secret, a choice must be made relatively soon after commercial use has begun. While secret or commercial use by someone having no association with the applicant will not bar the applicant from pursuing patent protection, secret use of an invention for commercial advantage by the applicant or someone in association with the applicant does bar the applicant from obtaining a patent if the period of use extends longer than one year.

While a United States patent application must be filed within one year of the initiation of secret use for commercial advantage, there is no limit on the length of time an invention may be used secretly before one files for patent protection in most foreign countries on the subject matter of the invention.

20-3 Bases of Protection. Trade secrets are not specifically protected by federal statutes. They are protected by state statutes, by principles of express or implied contract law, and the law of unfair competition. Trade secrets are based principally on the common law, as opposed to statutory law.

Several states impose criminal liability for misappropriation of trade secrets. Federal law makes it a crime to participate in interstate transportation of stolen trade secret material.

20-4   Protecting the Secrecy of Trade Secrets.   Since a trade secret must, by definition, remain a secret to be protectable, appropriate measures must be taken by the owner to maintain secrecy. If a company is to expect others to take its trade secrets seriously, a trade secret protection program needs to be set up with care to assure that all reasonable steps are taken to maintain the secrecy of the secrets. Employees should be put on notice that the company expects the trade secret information in their possession to be kept secret. Employees, manufacturer's representatives, consultants, and the like, should be bound to obligations of confidence. Visitor access to sensitive areas should be restricted, and visitors should be bound to obligations of confidence.

Obligations of confidentiality should also be included in dealings with suppliers, customers, and licensees. Confidential disclosures to third parties of trade secrets should be carefully documented. Those unto whom trade secrets are disclosed in confidence should be advised of their confidentiality obligations with respect to trade secret information, and should be asked to sign appropriate acknowledgements.

Since the character of a particular trade secret will do much to dictate the type of program that should be instituted to protect the integrity of the trade secret, no universally recognized procedures are applicable to all situations.

20-5   Employee Non-Competition Agreements.   Non-competition covenants in employee agreements restricting employees from competing with a trade secret holder after termination of employment will be enforced by courts only to the extent that these covenants are ancillary to a valid transaction or relationship, and to the extent they are reasonably limited in duration and geographic scope. A restrictive covenant must be necessary to the maintenance of trade secret advantages, and must be made in exchange for adequate consideration. Fresh consideration should be provided if a longstanding employee is asked for the first time to sign an agreement including a covenant not to compete.

REFERENCES

Callmann, Rudolf, *The Law of Unfair Competition, Trademarks and Monopolies*, Callaghan & Co., Chicago, 1967.

Chickering, Robert B., and Susan Hartman, *How to Register a Copyright and Protect Your Creative Work*, Scribner's Sons, New York, 1980.

Chisum, Donald S., *Patents*, Matthew Bender, New York, 1978, 1983.

Nimmer, Melville B., *Nimmer on Copyright*, Matthew Bender, New York, 1978.

Schwab, Arthur J., "Employee Agreements and Their Enforceability" in *Trade Secrets and Employment Agreements*, Virginia State Bar, Richmond, 1982.

Seidel, Arthur H., "The Law of Trade Secrets" in *Trade Secrets and Employment Agreements*, Virginia State Bar, Richmond, 1982.

PART FIVE

PRESERVING AND PROTECTING SPECIFIC TYPES OF INTELLECTUAL PROPERTY RIGHTS

CHAPTER TWENTY-ONE

Computerware

Protection of computer-related developments is a topic that merits special treatment. While the principles discussed in the foregoing chapters define the bases of available protections, this chapter illustrates their application. There are a variety of approaches that can be utilized to protect computerware. Often a combination of approaches is needed to achieve best results.

21-1 What is To Be Protected. Computerware takes a variety of forms. The term *computer software* includes computer programs, program descriptions, and supporting material. A *computer program* is a set of instructions, regardless of how expressed, that is capable, when incorporated in a machine-readable medium, of causing a machine or other device that has information processing capabilities to indicate, perform, or achieve a particular function, task, or result. A *program description* is a procedural representation in verbal, schematic, or other form, in sufficient detail to determine a set of instructions constituting a corresponding computer program. *Supporting material* is any material, other than a computer program or a program description, created for aiding the understanding or application of a computer program; for example descriptions and use instructions.

Copyright protection is available for all forms of computer software. If a work is originally authored, a copyright is born with the work. It should be preserved and protected through the use of proper copyright notices and by following deposit and registration procedures prescribed by the copyright law. Patent protection including apparatus and/or process claims may be available for a computer program if the invention criteria discussed in Chapter 4 are met.

The term *computer hardware* includes machines and other tangible devices which store, execute, display, output and communicate programs. Examples are memory systems, processing units, displays, keyboards, modems, and printers. Assuming the originality, novelty, utility, nonobviousness, and statutory bar requirements of patentable inventions are met, computer hardware is patentable.

21-2   Utility Patent Protection.   Patenting computer hardware has long been relatively easy in comparison with efforts to patent computer programs. Historically the Patent and Trademark Office has held that computer programs are not patentable. While the Office has advanced several reasons to support the nonpatentability of computer-related inventions, the crux of its position has been that computer programs do not constitute patentable subject matter.

While it has long been agreed that a program that seeks to protect nothing more than a mathematical formula and/or its use is not patentable, two Supreme Court cases have opened the way to patenting certain types of computer programs. *Diamond v. Brady,* 450 US 175, 101 S.Ct. 1495 (1981) and *Diamond v. Diehr,* 450 US 175, 101 S.Ct. 1048 (1981), make it clear that a computer program is not unpatentable simply because it is a computer program. A process claim that includes computational steps that are carried out by a computer may be patented, assuming it meets the other requirements of patentability set out in Chapter 4. Patentability was found in *Diehr* because the protection being sought was not directed simply to the use of an equation but rather to its use in conjunction with other steps of a claimed process.

Patent protection has the advantage of being relatively broad in its scope of protection as compared with other types of available protections. However, from a practical point of view, the pursuit of patents on software is deterred by relatively high costs both in obtaining and enforcing protection, and by a 24 to 48 month period during which an application is pending but no enforceable protection has issued.

21-3   Copyright Protection.   The Copyright Act of 1976 as amended by the Computer Software Act of 1980 clarified the copyright status of computer software. While the Copyright Office had begun accepting computer programs for registration in 1964, this was done under the "rule of doubt" whereby, if there is a doubt as to registrability, the Copyright Office opts to act in favor of registration. Now there is no question of the propriety of copyright registration regardless of whether a program is presented in object code or source code, and regardless of how the program is stored, for example on microchip, tape, or disk.

Copyright protection is obtained easily. Indeed, as is pointed out in greater detail in Chapter 19, it arises with the birth of an originally authored work, and covers even unpublished works. The concern an author usually faces is not how to obtain copyright rights, but rather how to keep from losing these rights.

Adequate and proper use of copyright notices is essential. Copyright notices should appear on the external label of a software cassette or disk, and on its packaging. Copyright notices should also appear on the first screen that appears when the program is run, in memory when the program is running, and within the first few lines when the program is printed.

A copyright protects the mode of expression of an idea, not the idea itself. An independently developed, noncopied presentation of an identical idea does not infringe one's copyright. As is discussed in greater detail in Chapter 19, if a few copies of a work such as a program have escaped without bearing proper notices, "saving provisions" of the new copyright law permit preservation of rights if one acts promptly.

While the new copyright law makes registration optional, it is desirable to proceed with registration promptly after publication, as discussed in Section 19-9, to avoid loss of rights such as an award of attorney's fees and statutory damages. As a minimum, the Copyright Office will require a deposit of the first and last 25 pages of the listing of a program when an application to register is filed.

21-4 Trade Secret Protection. Keeping a program secret prevents unauthorized use unless and until the secret escapes or the program is developed independently by another. Almost any form of development can be protected to a degree by keeping it secret, but outsiders cannot be prevented from using it if they develop the secret information independently or learn of it through lawful means. The biggest problem with trade secrets is the ease with which they can be lost, and hence the degree of care that must be taken to preserve secrecy.

Protection of trade secret rights in software should be implemented through a combination of suitable measures designed to prevent unauthorized access, discovery, and disclosure. Those who have access to trade secrets should be put on notice of the trade secret character of the material. Generous use of a "CONFIDENTIAL" label should be made on software and documents containing trade secrets. Employee and independent contractor agreements acknowledging duties of confidentiality are desirable to assure that these obligations are both understood and enforceable. Nondisclosure agreements binding outsiders to duties of confidentiality should be used with such outsiders as suppliers who have a need to know trade secret information.

21-5   Trademark Protection.   Trademarks enter the domain of computerware from the viewpoint of providing brand names for the marketing of products and services. Trademark protection for computerware itself is unavailable unless a product has a fanciful form that has become distinctive, as is discussed in Section 14-6.

21-6   Licensing.   As has been discussed in preceding chapters, almost all forms of intellectual property including patents, trademarks, copyrights, and trade secrets may be licensed to others in exchange for suitable consideration such as the payment of royalties. Usually one can charge whatever the market will bear as a license fee so long as antitrust liability does not arise from such activities as discriminatory licensing practices that hinder competition.

21-7   Copy Protection.   *Copy protection* is not a legally enforceable means of protecting software. Rather, it refers to the use of a stumbling block that hinders program duplication in operable form.

One problem with copy protection is that it is like using a lock to prevent unauthorized access; where there is a lock, there is a key that, when found, will open the lock. Another problem is the very understandable reluctance a potential customer has to buy a program he cannot readily copy to provide the backup that is needed in the event a malfunction renders the program original inoperable.

It does not constitute copyright infringement for the proper owner of a copy of a computer program to make or authorize the making of another copy or adaptation of the program, provided that the new copy or adaptation is created either:

1. As an essential step in the utilization of the computer program in conjunction with a machine, and that the copy or adaptation is used in no other manner, or

2. For archival purposes only, with all archival copies being destroyed in the event that continued possession of the computer program should cease to be rightful.

CHAPTER TWENTY-TWO

Biotechnology

Genetic engineering is forecast to be the biggest industry in America by 1990. At long last the path has been opened for inventors to obtain patent protection on manufactured life forms. This chapter explores such avenues as are open, and notes the surge of activity underway to preserve rights in one of our nation's most valuable areas of techno-logical expertise.

22-1 Recognizing the Urgency.   Biotechnology is not only a major hope for the future but also a fact of the present. Even as this is being written, developments are underway that, in relatively short periods of time, may provide a cure for cancer, an inexhaustible source of feedstock, and who knows what else. The stakes for those involved in biotechnology developments are enormous.

The promise of genetically enhanced microbes and enzymes for production of a host of chemicals, medicines, synthetic fuels, and new bacterial strains for performing all sorts of feats is so vast as to be incomprehensible. Within the next few years, almost anything that is basically a protein can be made in unlimited quantities by bacteria. Bacteria will be able to eat through oil spills and extract rare minerals from the earth. Indeed, what some have referred to as the "eighth day of creation" is at hand.

In the period of time before the Supreme Court ruled in favor of patentability for manufactured life forms, many articles were published expressing the urgent concern of scientists that unless patent protection was made available, scientists would be forced to operate in secrecy, which would set this area of technological development back many years. The need was made clear for patent protection to be made available so the fruits of research investments could be protected and so scientists could freely publish their discoveries.

While U.S. Patent 141,072 was granted in 1873 to Louis Pasteur covering a "yeast, free from organic germs of disease, as an article of manufacture," the patenting of life forms did not truly get a green light until the landmark Supreme Court decision of *Diamond v. Chakrabarty*, 447 U.S. 303, 206 USPQ 193 (1980). *Chakrabarty* struck down the position long propounded by the Patent and Trademark Office that patent law distinguishes between living and nonliving compositions of matter.

Since *Chakrabarty*, an unprecedented flood of applications relating to a single burgeoning area of technology has been received by the Patent and Trademark Office. Because the opportunity has been provided to write on an essentially clean slate, some of the protections being sought are quite broad in scope.

22-2   Available Types of Utility Patent Protection.   Assuming the originality, novelty, utility, nonobviousness, and statutory bar requirements of inventions as discussed in Chapter 4 are met, not only manufactured life forms but also their processes of manufacture and the uses to which they are put may be patented. Where composition of matter, process of production, and use protections are obtained, infringement will result if a third party:

1. Manufactures a patented life form using either a patented or an unpatented process
2. Manufactures an unpatented life form using a patented process
3. Imports a patented life form manufactured abroad using either a patented or unpatented process
4. Imports an unpatented life form manufactured abroad using a patented process, or
5. Uses a patented or unpatented life form for a patented purpose.

22-3   Applying for Patent Protection.   In order to comply with disclosure requirements of the patent law, special care needs to be taken in drafting a patent application to describe and characterize the organism being claimed. In order to comply with enablement and utility requirements of the law, an explanation should be included that not only delineates a careful description of the preferred use, but also explains the best mode known at the time an application is filed of creating the organism and putting the organism to use. A deposit of the organism in accordance with approved procedures will usually be required.

22-4   Foreign Patent Protection.   Patent protection similar to that now available in the United States is becoming progressively more available abroad. Canada now offers patent protection on life forms. Some limited protections are available in Japan.

A problem with laws of most foreign countries is that they do not allow the one year grace period provided by United States law to put a patent application on file after an invention has been made public. Hence, if one elects to publish the details of a discovery before putting at least a United States application on file, foreign protections may be lost, as is discussed in Chapter 12.

22-5   Trade Secret Protection.   In considering various options for protecting any type of intellectual property, the simple alternative of trade secret protection should be considered.

Rights in trade secrets have terms limited only by the degree to which secrecy can be maintained. If reverse engineering and independent development are not serious threats, if there is no desire to publish, and if secrecy can be upheld, trade secret protection of life forms can be very valuable indeed.

REFERENCES

Cooper, Iver P., *Biotechnology and the Law*, Clark Boardman, New York, 1982.

Plant, David W., Niels J. Reimers, and Norton D. Zinder, *Banbury Report*

10: Patenting of Life Forms, Cold Spring Harbor Laboratory, Cold Spring Harbor, NY, 1982.

Remer, Daniel, *Legal Care for Your Software*, Addison-Wesley, Reading, MA, 1982.

Soma, John T., *Computer Technology and the Law*, Shepard's/McGraw-Hill, Colorado Springs, 1983.

TYPICAL UTILITY PATENT

United States Patent [19]

Rampe

[11] **4,090,332**

[45] **May 23, 1978**

[54] **SUSPENSION SYSTEM FOR BOWL-TYPE VIBRATORY FINISHING MACHINE**

[75] Inventor: **John F. Rampe,** Mayfield Heights, Ohio

[73] Assignee: **Rampe Research,** Cleveland, Ohio

[21] Appl. No.: **720,212**

[22] Filed: **Sep. 3, 1976**

Related U.S. Application Data

[63] Continuation-in-part of Ser. No. 714,823, Aug. 16, 1976.

[51] **Int. Cl.²** **B24B 31/06**
[52] **U.S. Cl.** **51/163.2**
[58] **Field of Search** 51/163.1, 163.2

[56] **References Cited**

U.S. PATENT DOCUMENTS

3,449,869	6/1969	Rampe	51/163.1
3,708,918	1/1973	Pool	51/163.2
3,877,178	4/1975	Campanelli	51/163.2
3,991,524	11/1976	Ferrara	51/163.1

FOREIGN PATENT DOCUMENTS

1,652,154	5/1970	Germany	51/163.2

Primary Examiner—Harold D. Whitehead
Attorney, Agent, or Firm—David A. Burge Co.

[57] **ABSTRACT**

A vibratory finishing machine has a bowl structure supported by shear-loaded elastomeric mounts, and a drive system for vibrating the bowl structure about a node or null point located along a vertical center axis of the bowl structure. Each of the elastomeric mounts has one portion secured to the bowl structure, and another portion secured to a base structure. The one and another portions define an axis of each mount. Certain of the mounts are arranged such that their axes intersect the center axis above the node or null point. Others of the mounts are arranged such that their axes intersect the center axis below the node or null point. Mounts arranged as described stabilize the location of the node or null point and thereby render the machine less sensitive to variations in bowl loading.

22 Claims, 4 Drawing Figures

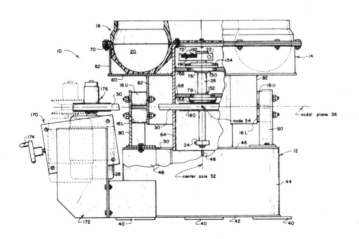

179

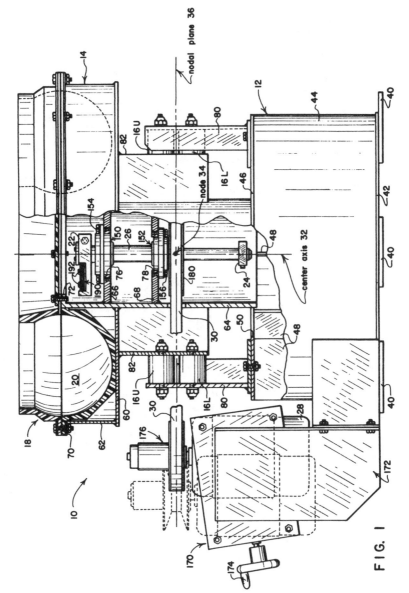

FIG. I

180

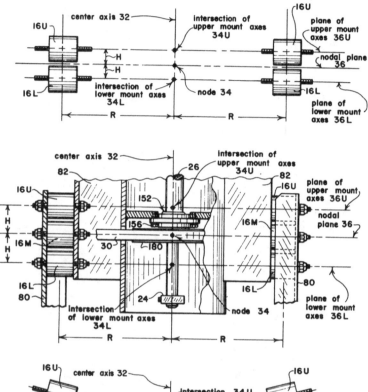

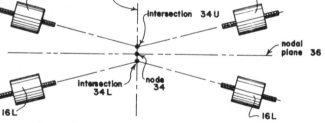

181

SUSPENSION SYSTEM FOR BOWL-TYPE VIBRATORY FINISHING MACHINE

REFERENCE TO RELATED AND RELEVANT PATENTS

The present application is a continuation-in-part of application Ser. No. 714,823, filed Aug. 16, 1976 and entitled Bowl-Type Vibratory Finishing Machine, here the "Bowl Machine Patent", the disclosure of which is incorporated by reference.

Molded Plastic Pulley With Heat Conducting Metal Lining, U.S. Pat. No. 3,142,997 issued Aug. 4, 1964 to J. F. Rampe, here the "Pulley Patent".

BACKGROUND OF THE INVENTION

1. Field of the Invention

The present invention relates generally to vibratory finishing machines, and more particularly to a novel and improved bowl-type vibratory finishing machine.

2. Prior Art

Many surface finishing operations such as deburring, burnishing, descaling, cleaning and the like can be conducted expeditiously in a vibratory finishing machine. Such a machine includes a movably mounted receptacle and a drive system for vibrating the receptacle. Workpieces to be finished are loaded into the receptacle together with finishing media. A finishing action is imparted to the workpieces by vibrating the receptacle so that the mixture of workpieces and media is effectively maintained in a fluid or mobile state with smaller components of the mixture dispersed between large components for impact. Impulse forces imparted to the mixture not only cause repeated impacts among its components but also cause the mixture to churn in a predictable manner as a finishing process is carried out.

Two basic types of vibratory finishing machines are in common use. One type employs an elongated, substantially horizontally disposed receptacle which is vibrated by eccentrics rotating about horizontal axes paralleling the length of the receptacle. This first type of machine is known in the art as a "tub-type mchine" or simply "tub machine", and its receptacle is commonly called a "tub". Another type uses a substantially annular receptacle which is vibrated by rotating one or more eccentrics about a vertical "center axis" located centrally of the receptacle when the receptacle is at rest. This latter type of machine is known in the art as a "bowl-type mchine" or simply "bowl machine", and its receptacle is commonly called a "bowl". While tub and bowl machines have many similar characteristics, they are sufficiently different in arrangement and operation that one will frequently offer advantages over the other in solving a particular finishing problem. The present invention relates to bowl-type machines.

During operation of a bowl machine, the bowl vibrates in gyratory movements about a node or null point located somewhere along the machine's center axis. This gyratory movement subjects the bowl's contents to a complex of vertical, radial and tangential impulse components which are intended to effect a uniform dispersion of the smaller components of the workpiece and media mixture among the large components of the mixture for impact. The resultant impulses are so oriented and timed as to cause both circumferential precession of the mixture and rotation of the mixture in essentially radiating vertical planes.

Those skilled in the art maintain different and conflicting theories on where the node or null point should be located along the center axis. Some maintain that the node or null point should be located within or near a horizontal plane which includes the center of gravity of the bowl's contents. This arrangement effectively minimizes horizontal impulse components imparted to the bowl's contents and maximizes the vertical components. Others maintain that a node or null point location slightly below the bottom of the bowl's chamber is desirable since it gives something of a mix of vertical, horizontal and tangential components. Still others advocate higher and lower node or null point locations.

Those skilled in the art similarly advance different and conflicting theories on the number of eccentrics which should be used to vibrate the bowl, the locations of the eccentrics, and the relative orientations of the eccentrics where more than one is used. Still other theories obtain on how and where a drive motor should connect with the eccentrics.

Factors such as node or null point location, the number, location and arrangement of eccentrics, and features of the drive motor connection all intertwine to determine such other factors as:

a. the simplicity or complexity of the machine;

b. the ease with which the machine can be serviced and such parts as bearings replaced;

c. the longevity of service which can be expected from the machine;

d. the sensitivity of the machine to different bowl loadings, i.e., whether it can handle a wide range of large and small, heavy and light loads; and

e. the type of vibratory movement which is imparted to the bowl, which, in turn, determines such things as:

 i. the type of circulation movement which will be executed by a mixture of media and workpieces in the bowl;

 ii. the direction and rate of precession of the mixture; and

 iii. the effectiveness of the resulting finishing action in terms of quality and time required to carry it out.

Previous proposals made in an effort to optimize these factors have resulted in machines which are relatively complex and difficult to service. The need for frequent bearing replacement has been a continuing problem, and the construction of many such machines has made bearing replacement difficult. Most bowl machines are quite sensitive to changes in bowl loading and operate effectively only in a relatively narrow loading range.

The invention described in the referenced Bowl Machine Patent addresses the foregoing and other problems of the prior art. It provides a bowl-type machine having a combination of features that are unique to the industry. The machine is of simple, relatively inexpensive construction. It has a relatively simple but rugged base structure, an equally simple and rugged bowl structure, and utilizes highly durable elastomeric mounts to support the bowl structure on the base structure.

A significant feature of the invention described in the Bowl Machine Patent lies in its novel arrangement of elastomeric mounts. Each mount has one portion secured to the base structure and another portion secured to the bowl structure. The one and another portions define an axis for each mount, and the mounts are arranged such that their axes intersect at a common point along the machine's center axis. The machine's drive

4,090,332

3

system is arranged to vibrate the tub about a node or null point which coincides with this common point. The arrangement of mounts assures that forces imposed on the mounts by movements of the bowl structure load the mounts in shear, i.e., in planes normal to their axes. When arranged and loaded in this manner, the mounts tend to resiliently oppose movements of the bowl structure in any mode other than about the desired node or null point. As a result, the machine is found to be substantially less sensitive to variations in receptacle loading than are other, previously proposed bowl-type machines. A single machine can, for example, handle bowl load volumes within as large a range as 2 cubic feet to 6 cubic feet, and is operable to impart a good finishing action to the load anywhere within this very broad range.

Bowl machine proposals prior to the invention described in the referenced Bowl Machine Patent do not address the problem of stabilizing actual node or null point location. It is believed that the tendency of node or null point location to vary with changes in bowl loading explains, at least in part, the difficulty prior proposals have encountered in providing machines that will handle a wide range of bowl loadings. If the actual location of the node or null point about which a bowl structure moves is displaced from the location for which the machine was designed, the machine operates inefficiently, if at all, and causes excessive wearing of drive and suspension system components.

SUMMARY OF THE INVENTION

The present invention provides a novel and improved suspension system for bowl-type vibratory finishing machines.

The invention described in the referenced Bowl Machine Patent and the present invention have several features in common. Both utilize an arrangement of elastomeric mounts to stabilize null point location and to thereby reduce the sensitivity of the machine to variation in bowl loading. Both inventions utilize mounts which are loaded principally by the dead weight of the bowl structure and its contents.

The inventions differ in their arrangement of mounts and the resulting loadings which are imposed on the mounts as their bowl structures move about their null points. Whereas the invention of the referenced Bowl Machine Patent addresses the problem of null point stability by providing an arrangement of elastomeric mounts having axes which intersect the machine's center axis at the desired null point location, the present invention provides even greater null point stability by using some mounts with axes which intersect the machine's center axis above the desired null point, and other mounts with axes which intersect the machine's center axis below the desired null point. Whereas the invention described in the referenced Bowl Machine Patent utilizes mounts loaded substantially solely in shear by vibratory movements of the bowl structure, the present invention utilizes mounts which are subjected to a degree of tensile and compressive loadings in a way which enhances null point stability.

In preferred practice, null point stability is enhanced through the use of upper and lower groups of mounts. The upper mounts have axes which extend in a first horizontal plane and intersect the machine's central axis a short distance "H" above the null point. The lower mounts have axes which extend in a second horizontal plane and intersect the machine's central axis at the

4

distance "H" below the null point. The same number of mounts are preferably included in each of the upper and lower groups, and each upper mount is preferably positioned in a vertically stacked arrangement directly above a separate one of the lower mounts. All of the mounts are preferably located at a common radial distance "R" from the machine's center axis.

The relationship of the "H" and "R" dimensions is selected such that while the mounts are loaded principally in shear by movements of the bowl structure, the mounts experience a degree of axial tension and compression. Inasmuch as the mounts oppose bowl structure movements which tend to axially strain the mounts, and inasmuch as movements of the bowl structure about the null point minimize axial mount strains, the mounts oppose movements of the bowl structure about any null points other than the null point.

As the bowl structure moves about the null point, each vertically stacked pair of upper and lower mounts will be cyclically axially loaded first with the upper mount in tension and the lower mount in compression, and then with the upper mount in compression and the lower mount in tension. The resistance offers by the mounts to axial extensions and compressions maintains the node point at a vertical location between the plane of the upper mount axes and the plane of the lower mount axes.

The described preferred arrangement of suspension system mounts can be used in combination with additional mounts having axes which intersect at the null point. Where such auxiliary mounts are used, the fact that their axes intersect at the null point assures that movements of the bowl structure about the null point will load the auxiliary mounts substantially solely in shear, whereby the chore of maintaining null point stability is left largely to the upper and lower mounts.

It is "unexpected", to say the least, that significant advantages in machine operating characteristics should result from the described relatively unorthodox arrangement of suspension system mounts. One would tend to think that all mount axes must necessarily intersect at the machine's null point for the machine to be operable. The present invention dispells this misconception and provides a novel approach to the problem of rendering a bowl-type vibratory finishing machine less sensitive to variations in bowl loading.

As will be apparent to those skilled in the art, once the concept of stabilizing null point location by utilizing the relative axial incompressibility and inextensibility of elastomeric mounts is recognized, a wide variety of mount arrangements utilizing this concept suggest themselves. Preferred arrangements are those wherein the mounts are subjected principally to shear loading by the dead weight of the bowl structure and its contents.

It is a general object of the present invention to provide a novel and improved bowl-type vibratory finishing machine.

It is another object to provide a bowl-type vibratory finishing machine having an improved suspension system.

It is still another object to provide a bowl-type finishing machine which is relatively insensitive to variations in bowl loading.

These and other objects and a fuller understanding of the invention described and claimed in the present application may be had by referring to the following description and claims taken in conjunction with the accompanying drawings.

4,090,332

5

BRIEF DESCRIPTION OF THE DRAWINGS

FIG. 1 is a side elevational view of a bowl-type vibratory finishing machine including one suspension system embodiment, the view having portions broken away and shown in cross-section, and showing in phantom one extreme position of a drive motor and variable speed pulley;

FIG. 2 is a schematic illustration of the suspension system employed in the machine of FIG. 1.

FIG. 3 is a view similar to FIG. 1 of an alternate suspension system embodiment; and,

FIG. 4 is a schematic illustration of still another suspension system embodiment.

DESCRIPTION OF THE PREFERRED EMBODIMENT

Referring to FIGS. 1 and 2, a vibratory finishing machine is indicated generally by the numeral 10. The machine 10 includes a base structure 12 and a bowl structure 14. Upper and lower sets of elastomeric mounts 16U, 16L resiliently interconnect the structures 12, 14 and permit relative movement therebetween. A replaceable liner assembly 18 forms part of the bowl structure 14 and defines an annular finishing chamber 20 for receiving media and workpieces to be finished. Vibratory movements are imparted to the bowl structure 14 by a drive system which includes a pair of eccentric weights 22, 24 supported on opposite ends of a rotatable shaft 26, a motor 28, and a belt 30 which drivingly interconnects the shaft 26 and the motor 28. The machine 10 is identical to the machine described in the referenced Bowl Machine Patent except for its arrangement of mounts 16U, 16L. The machine 10 has a "center axis", indicated by the numeral 32. The center axis 32 is an imaginary vertical line defined by the axis of the shaft 26 when the machine 10 is at rest. The center axis 32 extends substantially coaxially of the trough or chamber 20. During operation of the machine 10, the bowl structure 14 vibrates substantially about a node or null point 34. The node 34 is located at the juncture of the center axis 32 and a horizontally extending "nodal plane" 36. As will be appreciated by those skilled in the art, in actual practice the node or null point 34 is not a mathematical point but rather should be considered to be a small region around the juncture of the center axis 32 and the nodal plane 36. Depending on such variables as the position of the center of gravity of the bowl structure 14 and its contents, the node or null point 34 may be located a small distance above or below the nodal plane 36. Due to a number of factors including the fact that the bowl structure 14 need not be accurately balanced, the actual node or null point 34 may oscillate through small distances about the juncture of the center axis 32 and the nodal plane 36. As will be explained, the elastomeric mounts 16U, 16L serve to stabilize the location of the actual node or null point and to maintain it at the intersection of the center axis 32 with the nodal plane 36.

The base structure 12 has a welded framework including four feet 40, a bottom wall 42, a side wall 44, a top wall 46, and bracing plates 48. The feet 40 are welded to the underside of the bottom wall 42 and support the machine 10. The bottom wall 42 is a round plate which is perimetrically welded to the side wall 44. The side wall 44 is cylindrical and extends upwardly from the bottom wall 42. The top wall 46 is of annular configuration, is perimetrically welded to the side wall

6

44, and has a central opening 50. The bracing plates 48 are welded to the bottom and top walls 42, 46 to rigidify the framework formed by the bottom, side and top walls 42, 44, 46.

The bowl structure 14 has a welded framework including a bottom wall 60, a side wall 62, an upstanding center tube 64, and a pair of bearing mounting plates 66, 68. The bottom wall 60 is of annular configuration and is perimetrically welded to the side wall 62. The side wall 62 is of cylindrical configuration, extends upwardly from the bottom wall 60, and has a peripherally extending rim 70. The center tube 64 extends centrally through and is welded to the bottom wall 60. An inwardly turned rim 72 is formed on the upper end of the center tube, and the lower end of the center tube depends through the base structure opening 50. The bearing mounting plates 66, 68 are of annular configuration, are welded to the center tube 64, and have central openings 76, 78.

The elastomeric mounts 16U, 16L include four upper mounts 16U and four lower mounts 16L. The mounts 16U, 16L are preferably of a type sold by Lord Corporation, Erie, Pennsylvania, 16512, Part Number J5425-4, and have a spring rate of $K_r = 350$ pounds per inch. The mounts 16U, 16L interconnect four pairs of base and bowl structure brackets 80, 82. The mounts 16U, 16L are located symmetrically about the axis of the center tube 64 and overlie alternate ones of the bracing plates 48. The base structure brackets 80 are secured to the top wall 46 at locations above the bracing plates 48. The bowl structure 82 brackets are welded to the center tube 64.

FIG. 2 represents a schematic illustration of the suspension system mount arrangement employed in the machine 10. Referring to FIG. 2, the mounts 16U have axes which lie in a plane 36U above the nodal plane 36 and which intersect the center axis 32 at a point 34U above the node or null point 34. The mounts 16L have axes which lie in a plane 36L below the nodal plane 36 and which intersect the center axis 32 at a point 34L below the node or null point 34. The planes 36U, 36L parallel the nodal plane 36 and are spaced therefrom by a distance H. The mounts 16U, 16L are all located at equal radial distances from the center axis 32, as indicated by the dimensions "R".

Since the axes of the mounts 16U, 16L extend horizontally, the dead weight of the bowl structure 14 and its contents load the mounts 16U, 16L in shear. Since the axes of the mounts 16U, 16L pass quite closely by the node or null point 34, loads imposed on the mounts 16U, 16L by movements of the bowl structure 14 about the node or null point 34 are principally shear loads. But the fact that the mount axes do not pass directly through the node or null point 34 causes the mounts 16U, 16L to experience cylical compressive and tensile strains as the bowl structure 14 moves about the node or null point 34. Inasmuch as the mounts 16U, 16L strongly resiliently oppose being compressed and stretched in axial directions, they tend to confine movements of the bowl structure 14 to a mode where axial compressions and extensions of the mounts 16U, 16L are minimized. Since movements of the bowl structure 14 about the null point 34 minimize axial compressions and extensions of the mounts 16U, 16L, the described arrangement of mounts operates to confine movements of the bowl structure 14 to movements about the null point 34.

184

7

Stated in another way, an operating characteristic of the described suspension system is that it stabilizes the location of the actual node or null point about which the bowl structure 14 vibrates. Confining the movements of the bowl structure 14 in this manner is found to significantly reduce the sensitivity of the machine 10 to variations in finishing chamber loading. The operating characteristics of this suspension system are quite unlike previously proposed suspension systems which do little to assist in maintaining a constant node location to reduce sensitivity to variations in finishing chamber loading.

The shaft 26 is journaled by two bearing block assemblies 150, 152. The bearing assembly 150 extends through the mounting plate opening 76 and is secured to the mounting plate 66 by threaded fasteners 154. The bearing assembly 152 extends through the mounting plate opening 78 and is secured to the mounting plate 68 by threaded fasteners 156.

The motor 28 is movably supported by a conventional, adjustable motor mount 170. A bracket assembly 172 supports the motor mount 170 and the base structure 12. The mount 170 has a crank 174 which can be turned to move the motor 28 inwardly and outwardly toward and away from the shaft 26. A variable diameter pulley 176 of the type described in the referenced Pulley Patent is supported on the drive shaft of the motor 28. When the motor 28 is at the inward end of its range of travel, the pulley 176 has a relatively large effective outer diameter, as shown in solid lines in FIG. 1. When the motor 28 is at the outward end of its range of travel, the pulley 176 has a relatively small effective outer diameter, as shown in phantom in FIGS. 1 and 2.

A fixed diameter pulley 180 is secured to the lower end region of the shaft 26. The belt 30 is reeved around and drivingly interconnects the pulleys 176, 180. Depending on the position of the motor 28, the belt 30 is operable to drive the shaft at speeds with the range of about 700 to 1450 revolutions per minute.

A feature of the machine 10 is that the pulleys 176, 180 and the drive belt 30 are located in the nodal plane 36. This arrangement minimizes radial movements of the pulley 180 during machine operation and thereby overcomes problems of excessive belt wear, stretching and failure encounteded in many previously proposed bowl machines.

The eccentric 22 carries a plurality of removable weights 190 which are held in place by threaded fasteners 192. The weights 190 can be added and removed as required to accommodate exceptionally large or small loads of workpieces and finishing media and to adjust the machine for optimal operation within the loading range most commonly used by a particular customer.

Referring to FIG. 3, the upper and lower mounts 16U, 16L can be augmented with a third group of mounts 16M. Each of the mounts 16M is located between a separate pair of upper and lower mounts 16U, 16L and has its axis in the nodal plane 36. Since axes of the mounts 16M intersect at the node or null point 34, the mounts 16M are loaded substantially exclusively in shear by movements of the bowl structure 14 about the node or null point 34.

In mount arrangements where the axes of the upper and lower mounts lie in planes which parallel the nodal plane (i.e., the arrangements of FIGS. 1–3), the dimensions H and R must be selected with care to assure that the distance H does not become too large in comparison with the dimension R. A preferred relationship of the

8

dimensions H and R is about $H = 0.12R$. As H is decreased below 0.12R, the null point stabilization effect provided by the upper and lower mounts diminishes because these mounts are subjected to less axial strain as the bowl structure 14 moves about the node or null point 34. As H is increased beyond 0.12R, the magnitude of the null point stabilization effect increases rapidly and requires substantially larger drive system power inputs to vibrate the bowl structure 14. In short, selecting a relationship between the dimensions H and R involves a compromise between the desirability of stabilizing null point location, and the desirability of keeping power input requirements minimal.

While horizontally-oriented mount axis arrangements of the types shown in FIGS. 1 – 3 are preferred, other less preferred arrangements can be used which incorporate certain principles of the present invention. Referring to FIG. 4, one such arrangement includes inclined upper and lower mounts 16U, 16P having axes intersection points 34U, 34L. This type of mount arrangement is not preferred inasmuch as the mounts 16U, 16L are not loaded solely in shear by the dead weight of the bowl and structure 14 and its contents. Other arrangements of mounts having axis intersection points above and below the node 34 can also be used, together with, or without, still other mounts whose axes intersect the node 34.

As will be apparent from the foregoing description, the present invention provides a novel and improved bowl-type machine of simple construction which is relatively insensitive to variations in bowl loading and which includes a suspension system that greatly enhances null point stability. The principles of this invention can be applied to larger and smaller bowl type machines by using mount arrays which include larger and smaller numbers of elastomeric mounts.

Although the invention has been described in its preferred form with a certain degree of particularity, it is understood that the present disclosure of the preferred form has been made only by way of example and numerous changes in the details of construction and the combination and arrangement of parts may be resorted to without departing from the spirit and scope of the invention as hereinafter claimed. It is intended that the patent shall cover, by suitable expression in the appended claims, whatever features of patentable novelty exist in the invention disclosed.

I claim:

1. A bowl-type vibratory finishing machine, comprising:

a. a base structure;

b. a bowl structure having a central axis and defining a substantially annular chamber adapted to receive finishing media and workpieces to be finished;

c. a plurality of elastomeric mounts movably supporting the bowl structure on the base structure, each of the mounts having one portion secured to the bowl structure and another portion secured to the base structure, the one and another portions defining an axis for each mount;

d. drive means for vibrating the bowl structure relative to the base structure to impart a finishing action to contents of the chamber with the bowl structure moving substantially about a nodal point on the central axis;

e. the elastomeric mounts including a first group of mounts arranged such that their axes intersect at the central axis at a first location on one side of the nodal point, and a second group of mounts arranged such that their axes intersect the central axis at a second location on the other side of the nodal point.

2. The bowl type vibratory finishing machine of claim 1 wherein the elastomeric mounts of one of the groups are arranged with their axes in a common, first horizontal plane.

3. The bowl-type vibratory finishing machine of claim 2 wherein the elastomeric mounts of the other of the groups are arranged with their axes in a common, second horizontal plane.

4. The bowl-type vibratory finishing machine of claim 1 wherein the elastomeric mounts include a third group of mounts arranged such that their axes intersect the central axis substantially at the nodal point.

5. The bowl-type vibratory finishing machine of claim 4 wherein the elastomeric mounts of the third group are arranged with their axes in a common, horizontal plane which includes the nodal point.

6. The bowl-type vibratory finishing machine of claim 1 wherein each group includes at least three mounts.

7. The bowl-type vibratory finishing machine of claim 6 wherein the first and second groups each consist of the same number of mounts.

8. The bowl-type vibratory finishing machine of claim 7 wherein each mount of the first group overlies a separate one of the mounts of the second group.

9. The bowl-type vibratory finishing machine of claim 1 wherein certain of the elastomeric mounts are located at substantially equal distances from the central axis.

10. The bowl-type vibratory finishing machine of claim 1 wherein the distance between the first location and the nodal point equals the distance between the second location and the nodal point.

11. A bowl-type vibratory finishing machine, comprising:
a. a base structure;
b. a bowl structure;
c. first and second groups of elastomeric mounts movably supporting the bowl structure on the base structure;
d. each group of mounts including at least three mounts;
e. each of the mounts having one portion secured to the bowl structure and another portion secured to the base structure, the one and another portions defining an axis for each mount;
f. the mounts of the first group having axes which intersect at a first point;
g. the mounts of the second group having axes which intersect at a second point spaced from the first point; and,
h. drive means for vibrating the bowl structure relative to the base structure substantially about a

nodal point located between the first and second points.

12. The bowl-type vibratory finishing machine of claim 11 wherein the nodal point is located substantially equidistant from the first and second points.

13. The bowl-type vibratory finishing machine of claim 11 additionally including a third group of mounts arranged such that their axes intersect substantially at the nodal point.

14. The bowl-type vibratory finishing machine of claim 11 wherein the first and second groups each consist of the same number of mounts.

15. The bowl-type vibratory finishing machine of claim 14 wherein each mount of the first group overlies a separate one of the mounts of the second group.

16. A bowl-type vibratory finishing machine, comprising:
a. a base structure;
b. a bowl structure;
c. drive means for vibrating the bowl structure relative to the base structure substantially about a null point;
d. shear-loaded elastomeric mount means including a plurality of elastomeric mounts for movably supporting the bowl structure on the base structure, the mounts being relatively incompressible and inextensible under the influence of compression and tension forces; and,
e. mounting means arranged and supporting selected ones of the mounts for utilization of the relatively incompressible and inextensible nature thereof to stabilize the location of the null point as the bowl structure vibrates relative to the base structure.

17. The bowl-type vibratory finishing machine of claim 16 wherein each of the mounts has one portion secured to the bowl structure and another portion secured to the base structure, the one and another portions defining an axis for each mount, and the axes of the selected mounts do not intersect the null point.

18. The bowl-type vibratory finishing machine of claim 17 wherein the axes of mounts other than the selected mounts intersect the null point.

19. The bowl-type vibratory finishing machine of claim 17 wherein the selected mounts include first and second groups of mounts, the mounts of the first group having axes which intersect on one side of the null point, and the mounts of the second group having axes which intersect on the other side of the null point.

20. The bowl-type vibratory finishing machine of claim 19 wherein each mount of the first group overlies a separate one of the mounts of the second group.

21. The bowl-type vibratory finishing machine of claim 19 wherein each group includes at least three mounts.

22. The bowl-type vibratory finishing machine of claim 21 wherein the first and second groups each consist of the same number of mounts.

* * * * *

TYPICAL DESIGN PATENT

United States Patent [19]

Burge

[11] **Des. 251,223**

[45] ** **Mar. 6, 1979**

[54] **COMBINED HAT AND COAT RACK**

[76] Inventor: **David A. Burge**, 3594 Glencairn Rd., Shaker Heights, Ohio 44122

[**] Term: **14 Years**

[21] Appl. No.: **786,300**

[22] Filed: **Apr. 11, 1977**

[51] **Int. Cl.** .... **D6—04**
[52] **U.S. Cl.** **D6/116**; D6/114; D6/132
[58] **Field of Search** .... D6/114, 116, 120, 124, D6/125, 129, 130, 132, 134, 136; 211/60 R, 87, 90, 100, 135; 248/309 R, 310, 311.1, 312, 315; 108/27, 152; 242/134; 223/106

[56]   **References Cited**

U.S. PATENT DOCUMENTS

D. 137,159	2/1944	Borah	D6/124
560,923	5/1896	Peter	211/87
797,614	8/1905	Schipkowsky	211/87

FOREIGN PATENT DOCUMENTS

238489	7/1945	Switzerland	211/90

Primary Examiner—Wallace R. Burke
Assistant Examiner—B. J. Bullock
Attorney, Agent, or Firm—David A. Burge

[57]   **CLAIM**

The ornamental design for a combined hat and coat rack, as shown.

DESCRIPTION

FIG. 1 is a perspective view of a combined hat and coat rack showing my new design;

FIG. 2 is an enlarged front elevational view of FIG. 1;

FIG. 3 is a side elevational view of FIG. 2;

FIG. 4 is a rear elevational view of FIG. 2.

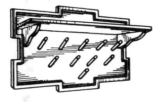

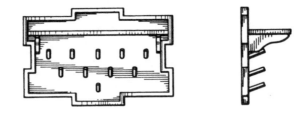

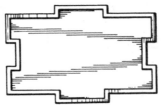

TYPICAL TRADEMARK REGISTRATIONS

Int. Cl.: 4

Prior U.S. Cl.: 15

United States Patent and Trademark Office

Reg. No. 1,095,650
Registered July 11, 1978

TRADEMARK
Principal Register

BLAK-GARD

Complete Coatings Corporation (Ohio corporation)
9107 Frederick Ave.
Cleveland, Ohio 44104

For: PHOSPHATE AND LUBRICANT TYPE COAT-
ING COMPOSITION MATERIALS, in CLASS 4 (U.S.
CL. 15).

First use at least as early as Dec. 1, 1976; in commerce
at least as early as Dec. 1, 1976.

Ser. No. 117,589, filed Mar. 1, 1977.

Int. Cl.: 40

Prior U.S. Cl.: 106

United States Patent and Trademark Office

Reg. No. 1,104,956

Registered Oct. 24, 1978

SERVICE MARK
Principal Register

BLAK-GARD

Complete Coatings Corporation (Ohio corporation)
9107 Frederic Ave.
Cleveland, Ohio 44104

For: PROTECTIVELY FINISHING FERROUS-BASED METAL PRODUCTS BY APPLYING A PHOSPHATE AND LUBRICANT COATING, in CLASS 40 (U.S. CL. 106).

First use at least as early as Dec. 1, 1976; in commerce at least as early as Dec. 1, 1976.

Ser. No. 163,279, filed Mar. 23, 1978.

Int. Cl.: 6

Prior U.S. Cl.: 13

United States Patent and Trademark Office

Reg. No. 1,112,606
Registered Feb. 6, 1979

TRADEMARK
Principal Register

BLAK-GARD

Complete Coatings Corporation (Ohio corporation)
9107 Frederick Ave.
Cleveland, Ohio 44104

For: PHOSPHATE AND LUBRICANT COATINGS SOLD AS AN INTEGRAL PART OF HARDWARE, in CLASS 6 (U.S. CL. 13).

First use at least as early as Dec. 1, 1976; in commerce at least as early as Dec. 1, 1976.

Ser. No. 163,318, filed Mar. 23, 1978.

GLOSSARY

APPLICANT One who files an application with a governmental body seeking protection for, or registration of, intellectual property rights.

ASSIGNEE One who receives intellectual property rights by assignment.

ASSIGNMENT A transfer of ownership rights in intellectual property.

ASSIGNOR One who conveys intellectual property rights to another by assignment.

CLAIM A single-sentence paragraph presented toward the end of a patent application or patent, defining one set of limits or boundaries of the invention described in the application or patent.

COMMON LAW Principles and rules of law not codified by statute, but promulgated through court decisions.

CONCEPTION The initial mental formulation of the essential elements of an invention.

CONTINUATION A patent application filed during the pendency of an earlier-filed application containing claims to the same invention as that claimed in the earlier-filed application.

CONTINUATION-IN-PART A patent application filed during the pendency of an earlier-filed application repeating some substantial portion of that application and adding new matter not disclosed in it.

CONTRIBUTORY INFRINGEMENT The intentional aiding of another in the direct infringement of a patent by selling one or more material elements of the patented invention when the elements are not staple articles of commerce.

DILIGENCE   Vigilant, continuing activity such as that which follows conception and leads to the reduction to practice of an invention, or that which leads to a constructive reduction to practice as by filing a patent application.

DISCLAIMER, STATUTORY   A dedication to the public of one or more of the claims of a patent.

DISCLAIMER, TERMINAL   A dedication to the public of a portion of the term of a patent.

DISCLOSURE   A means by which the subject matter of an invention is revealed to another.

DIVISION   A patent application filed during the pendency of an earlier-filed application presenting claims to subject matter described, but not (or no longer) claimed in the earlier-filed application.

EMBODIMENT   One specific form of practicing an invention.

EXAMINER   An employee of the United States government charged with examining patent, trademark, or copyright applications.

FILE WRAPPER   The file maintained by the Patent and Trademark Office containing all papers that form the history of examination of a particular application.

INDUCING INFRINGEMENT   Enticing another to directly infringe a patent.

INFRINGER   One who wrongfully treads on the intellectual property rights of another by appropriating another's invention, copying another's copyrighted work, using another's trademark, and the like.

INTERFERENCE   A Patent and Trademark Office proceeding intended to determine which of two inventors should be entitled to pursue a patent on an invention.

ISSUANCE   The granting of a patent, a trademark registration, or a copyright registration.

LICENSE   A transfer of intellectual property rights other than ownership.

LICENSEE   One who receives intellectual property rights by license.

LICENSOR One who conveys intellectual property rights to another by license.

NEW MATTER Subject matter above and beyond that originally presented in a patent application.

PATENTEE An inventor who has been granted a patent.

PATENT OWNER One who owns all rights in a patent, either a patentee or an assignee.

PENDENCY The period of time beginning with the time an application is filed and terminating with either the abandonment of the application or its issuance as a patent, a trademark registration, or a copyright registration.

PRIOR ART That which is known to the public prior to the date in question.

REDUCTION TO PRACTICE, ACTUAL The act of completing an invention and testing it as may be required to assure that it is operable under typical conditions of service.

REDUCTION TO PRACTICE, CONSTRUCTIVE The act of filing a patent application that includes a complete description of an operable invention.

SPECIFICATION That portion of a patent application describing and defining an invention in written terminology.

WORKING REQUIREMENT The requirement of a foreign country necessitating that an invention be practiced or licensed in such country to maintain the patent in force.

Index

Abandoned applications, retained in
    secrecy, 59
  access by petition, 59
Abandonment:
  invention, 39, 41
  patent application, 59, 62, 63
  trademark, 126
Access to pending patent application,
    59
Actual reduction to practice, 33, 85
Affidavit:
  overcoming rejection of claimed
    invention in patent application,
    63
  trademark continued use, 136, 137
  trademark incontestability, 138, 139
Affiliate, definition for small entity
    status determination, 56, 57
Agencies, governmental, 5–7
Agents, patent, 19
Alloys, 35
Allowance:
  notice of, 61, 64, 67
  of patent, 61, 64, 67
Amendment in patent prosecution, 62,
    63
Anderson's-Black Rock, Inc. v.
    Pavement Salvage Co., Inc., 43,
    44
Anticipation, invention, 38–41
Antitrust:
  licensing restrictions, 106, 107
  violations as defense to patent
    enforcement, 76, 77

Appeal in patent application
    prosecution, 64
Applicant, 35, 36
Application:
  abandonment, 59, 62, 63
  changing content after execution, 54
  content, utility patent, 48–53
  continuation, 68, 69
  continuation-in-part, 68, 69
  declaration, 53, 54
  design patent, *see* Design patent
  division, 68, 69
  drawing, *see* Drawing
  execution, 53, 54
  file history, 67
  file wrapper, 67
  filing date, 55, 57
  filing fee:
    design patent application, 55
    trademark application, 136
    utility patent application, 54, 55
  fraud in prosecution, 60
  notice of allowance, 61, 64, 67
  oath, 53, 54
  patent, *see* Design patent; Utility
    patent
  prosecution:
    design application, 147
    trademark application, 136–138
    utility application, 58–69
  secrecy, 58, 59
  striking from PTO records, 60
  utility patent, *see* Utility patent
Arbitrary mark, 124

Arbitration of patent-related disputes, 80
Articles of manufacture, as statutory class of patentable subject matter, 34–36
Assignee:
  issuance of patent to, 105
  prosecution of patent application by, 104
Assignment:
  copyright, 159
  employee invention rights, 103–105
  patent and/or patent application, 102–104
  recording in Copyright Office, 159
  recording in Patent and Trademark Office, 102, 103, 106, 140
  trademark, 140
Atomic energy related inventions, 36
Attorney, patent, 19
  conflict of interest, 20
  directory, 19
  in-house, 21, 22
  selection, 19–20
  services, 18
  Yellow Pages listing, 19

Benefits of patent systems, 32
Best mode requirement, 50, 51
Biotechnology, 172–175
  applying to protect, 174
  foreign protection, 174
  life forms protection, 172, 173
  trade secret protection, 174
  urgency to protect, 172
  utility patent protection, 173, 174
Board of Appeals, 64

Canada:
  industrial design registration, 10
  patent filing, 109
Cancellation of trademark registration, 138, 139
Candor, duty of, 59, 60
Cease and desist letter, 29

Certificate of correction, 67, 68
Certificate of Express Mailing, 57
Certificate of Plant Variety Protection, 7, 151
  rights granted, 151
  term, 151
Certification mark, 10, 114
Chain of applications, 69
Chair, Parable of the, 27–29
Changing application after execution, 54
Claim:
  amendment, 62, 63
  body portion, 52
  dependent, 52, 53
  design patent, 146
  disclaiming invalid, 73, 74
  format, 51–53
  functional language, 51, 52
  importance, 49
  independent, 52, 53
  interpretation of claims, 62
    doctrine of equivalents, 74
    in light of file history, 62, 67, 76
  Jepson-type, 53
  means-plus-function language, 51, 52
  multiple dependent, 53
  new matter, 63
  preamble portion, 52
  product-by-process, 52, 53
  transition portion, 52
  types, 51–53
Classification:
  patents, 14
  trademarks, 136
Coined mark, 124, 126
Collective mark, 10, 114
Combination of references, 39, 41–44
Combination patent, 44
Commerce, trademark use in, 133
Commercial mark, 10
Composition of matter, as statutory, 34–36
  class of patentable subject matter, 34–36

Compounds, 34–36
Computerware, 167–171
  copy protection of programs, 170,
    171
  copyright protection, 167–169
  hardware, 168
    patent protection, 168
    trade secret protection, 167
    types of, 168
  licensing, 170
  patent protection, 168
  program, 167
    copy protection, 170, 171
    patent protection, 168
    trade secret protection, 167, 169,
     170
  software, 167
    patent protection, 168
    trade secret protection, 167
    types of, 167
  trademark protection, 170
  trade secret protection, 167
Concealment of invention, 38, 39, 41
Conception of invention, 33, 84–86
  documenting, 82, 83
Confidential, disclosure agreement,
  96–98
  drawing notice, 94
  information guarding, 92
  relationship in disclosing invention,
   96–98
  trade secrets, 163
Constitution, Article I, Section 8, 32
  supports copyright protection, 120,
   152
  supports patent protection, 32, 120
Constructive reduction to practice, 33
Continuation application, 68, 69
Continuation-in-part application, 68, 69
Contractual view of patents, 25
Copy protection of computer programs,
  170, 171
Copyright, 11, 12
  Act of 1976, 152, 154, 156–158
  application forms, 156

  assignment of, 159
  character of rights, 152–159
  constitutional basis, 32, 120, 152
  deposit requirement, 157, 158
  designs, 147, 148
  expedited registration handling, 156
  fair use of copyrighted work, 158
  fees, 156
  notice, 157
    computerware, use on, 168, 169
    content, 157
    form, 157
    position, 157
  number of registrations, 11
  protection of computerware, 168,
   169
  registration benefits, 159
  registration procedure, 155, 156
  relationship to design patents, 147,
   148
  relationship to patents, 152, 153
  relationship to trademarks, 119, 120
  requirements of authorship, fixation,
   originality, 153, 154
  saving provisions of law, 158
  subject matter of, 154, 155
  term, 11, 156, 157
  unpublished work, 152, 159
  work for hire, 154
Copyright Office, 6, 7
  works deposited in, 6, 157, 158
Correction of error in patent, 67, 68
  by certificate of correction, 67, 68
  by reissue, 71–73
Correction of inventorship, 37, 38
Court of Appeals for the Federal
  Circuit, 43, 44, 77, 78
Court of Customs and Patent Appeals,
  77
Covenant not to sue, 108
Cross-licensing of patents, 31
Customer list, as trade secret, 160

Damages:
  recovery in design patent suit, 147

Damages (*Continued*)
recovery in patent suit, 78
recovery in trademark suit, 141, 142
Date, filing by Express Mail, 57
Deadline for responding to PTO
communication, 63
Declaration, patent application, 53, 54
Declaratory judgment, 79
Defenses to patent infringement, 76, 77
Defensive publication program, 6
Delay, detrimental, 17, 18
Department of Agriculture, 7
Deposit requirement, copyright, 157, 158
Description requirement, 50, 51
Descriptive mark, 125
Designing around infringement
concerns, 90
Design patent, 8, 10, 145–149
application content, 146, 147
Canadian, 10
claim, 146
copyright overlap, 147, 148
drawing, 146
enforcement, 147
example of, Appendix Two
foreign protection, 8, 13
infringement, 147
number of patents issued, 6
prosecution, 147
relationship to copyrights, 147, 148
relationship to trademarks, 148, 149
requirement of ornamentality, 145
requirements of novelty and
nonobviousness, 145
term, 8, 147
trademark overlap, 148, 149
Diamond v. *Brady*, 168
Diamond v. *Chakrabarty*, 173
Diamond v. *Diehr*, 168
Diligence:
documentation of, 86, 87
priority of invention, 86, 87

*Directory of Registered Patent
Attorneys and Agents*, 19
Disclaimer:
statutory, 73, 74
terminal, 67
Disclosure:
content, 82–87
duty to PTO, 54
format, 83–86
signing and dating, 82, 83
witnesses, 82, 83
Disclosure document, 99–101
Disclosure Document Program, 6, 100, 101
Disclosure statement, information, 59, 60
Distinctiveness, trademark, 120, 121, 126
Distinctness requirement of invention
for patentability, 50, 51
Division application, 68, 69
Doctrine of Equivalents, 74
Documents, missing or misfiled, 47
Double patenting, 66, 67
Drawing:
confidentiality notice, 94
content, design application, 146
correction by bonded drafting
service, 63
correction by submitting substitutes, 63
trademark application, 127
utility application, 49, 50
Duty of candor, 54
dealing with Patent and Trademark
Office, 54
fraud consequence of failure to meet, 60
information disclosure statement, 60

Election requirement, 62, 63
request for reconsideration, 66
traversing, 66

Employee:
  agreement to maintain secrecy, 163
  assignment of invention rights, 103,
    104
  creation of work for hire, 153, 154
  encouraging creative contributions
    of, 92
  non-competition agreements, 163,
    164
  release of invention rights from
    employer, 104
Enablement requirement, 50, 51
Equivalents, doctrine of, 74
Error in patent, correction of, 67, 68
European Patent Convention, 112,
  113
Examiner, 6
  commenting on reasons for allowing
    patent issuance, 64, 65
  interviewing, 65
  number of, 6
Examiners' art, 47
Example:
  design patent, Appendix Two
  trademark registrations, Appendix
    Three
  utility patent, Appendix One
Execution of application, 53, 54
Ex parte Jepson, 53
Experimental use, 44, 45
Express Mail filing, 57
Extension of time in patent
  prosecution, 63

Fees, 54–57
  design patent application, 55
  filing, 55, 136
  foreign, 110
  issue, utility patent, 55
  maintenance, 55, 56
  refund of excessive fee payment, 57
  small entity status reduction, 56, 57
  trademark application, 136
  utility patent, 55, 56
  utility patient application, 55

Fictitious name, 11
  definition, 11
  registration, 11
File history, 62, 67
File wrapper, 62, 67
Filing date, 57, 58, 111
Filing by Express Mail, 57
Filing receipt, 36
  granting of license to file abroad, 36
Final rejection:
  available options upon receipt of, 64
  when issued, 62, 64
Firm name registration, 5, 11
First action allowance of all claims, 61
Fixation requirement, 153, 154
Fleming, Sir Alexander, 26, 27
Foreign filing, 8, 13
  Canada, 10, 109
  country by country, 111
  European Patent Convention, 112,
    113
  high cost of, 109–113
  international convention, 110, 111
  license, 36
  Paris Convention, 110
  Patent Cooperation Treaty, 111,
    112
  tax payments, 110
Franchising, 11
Fraud:
  consequences of, 76, 77
  as defense, in patent litigation, 76,
    77
  small entity status improperly
    established, 57
Functional language in patent claims,
  51, 52

Game, protecting various aspects of, 4,
  5
Goodwill associated with trademark,
  120, 121
Governmental agencies, 5–7
Graham v. John Deere, 43
Grant character of patent, 25–29

Humanitarian misconceptions of
    patents, 26, 27

Ideas:
    relationship to inventions, 33, 34
    submission to others, 30, 31
Incontestability of trademark
    registration, 138, 139
Indefiniteness objections to content of
    application, 61
Independent inventor, 56
Information Disclosure Statement, 59,
    60
    Patent Office guidelines for
        preparing and filing, 59
Infringement:
    avoiding, 18, 89–92
    contributory, 74
    defenses to, 76, 77
    deliberate, 90, 91
    direct, 74
    failure to sue for, 79
    inducement of, 74
    notice, importance of, 70, 71
    search, 89
    suit, 75–80
In-house counsel, 21, 22
Intellectual property, 3–5, 12, 13
Interference, 80, 81
    diligence documentation, 86, 87
International application, 113, 114
    European Patent Convention, 112,
        113
    Patent Cooperation Treaty, 111, 112
International Convention, 110, 111
International patent protection,
    110–114
    advantages and disadvantages, 113,
        114
    European Patent Convention, 112,
        113
    Patent Cooperation Treaty, 111, 112
    trends, 114
Interview with examiner, 65

Invention:
    agreement with employee, 103, 114
    conception, 33
    confidential disclosure to protect
        rights, 97, 98
    definition, 33
    marketing firms, 98–100
    notebook, 83–85
    patentable, 33, 34
    priority of, 81
    records, 82–87
    reduction to practice, 33
    relation to ideas, 33, 34
Inventorship:
    correction of, 37, 38
    joint, 37
    misjoinder of, 37, 38
    nonjoinder of, 37, 38
    originality requirement, 37, 38
    sole, 37
Issuance of patent to assignee, 105
Issue fee:
    design application, 55, 56
    establishing small entity status
        before paying, 55–57
    utility application, 55, 56

Jepson-type claims, 53
Joinder of inventors, 37, 38
Joint inventorship, 37

Kewanee Oil v. *Bicron Corp.*, 34
Know-how, 7, 12

Lanham Act, 134
Law of nature, 35
Library of Congress, 6, 7
    copyright deposits to, 6
License:
    antitrust complications, 106, 107
    cross-license, 31
    exclusive, 106
    foreign filing, 36
    nonexclusive, 105, 106

recording of, 106
shopright as, 105
sublicense provision, 107, 108
typical provisions, 107, 108
Likelihood of confusion, 123, 124
Litigation:
declaratory judgment, 79
defenses in patent suit, 76, 77
expense of patent suit, 75
failure to sue infringers, 79, 80
institution of patent suit, 75
obtaining damages, 78
settling, 78, 79
uniformity of court decisions in
patent cases, 77, 78
Look-alike products, 128–130
trademark infringement, 141, 142
unfair competition, 117

Machine, as statutory class of
patentable subject matter,
34–36
Mailing by Express Mail of papers, 57
Maintenance fees, 55, 56
foreign patent, 110
small entity status reduction, 56
utility patent, 55, 56
Manufacture, as statutory class of
patentable subject matter,

Mark, commercial, 10
Marketing:
detrimental delay, 17, 18
invention promoters, 98–100
techniques for, 96–98
Marking:
compliance with federal laws, 58, 59,
70, 71
Customs checking of, 131
false, 58, 59, 70, 71
Federal Trade Commission checking
of, 131
foreign origin, 130–131
patent, 58, 59, 70, 71

Material, as term is applied to facts
that should be disclosed, 60
Means-plus-function claim language,
51, 52
Mental step, process involving, 35
Method of conducting business, 35
Misconceptions, patent grant, 25–27
Misjoinder of inventors, 37, 38
Misuse:
patent, 76, 77
trademark, 123–128
Mixture of ingredients, 35
Monopoly:
relationship to patent, 26
relationship to trademarks, 117, 118
Monopoly, loss of this trademark, 118,
119

Naked license of trademark, 141
Name:
fictitious, 11
partnership, 5, 11
right to control use of personal, 13
trade, 5, 11
Negative character of patent grant,
27–29
Negative rules of invention, 38
New matter, 63
Nonjoinder of inventors, 37, 38
Nonobviousness, 41–44
in design cases, 145
in utility cases, 41–44
secondary considerations, 43, 44
evidence, 43
when considered, 43
synergism, 43, 44
statutory basis, 42
Nonprofit organization, entitled to
small entity status benefits, 56,
57
Notebook, invention, 83–85
Notice of Allowance, 61, 64, 67
accompanied by statement of reasons
for allowance, 64

Notice of Issuance, 67
Notice of patent infringement, 70, 71
Novelty requirement of patent law,
    38–41

Oath in patent application, 53, 54
Objection in patent prosecution, 61
Obviousness, *see* Nonobviousness
Office Action, patent, 60–67
    amending claims in responding, 63
    arguing for allowance in responding,
        63
    cancellation of claims in responding,
        63
    content:
        including objection to drawings,
            62, 63
        including objection to informality,
            63
        including rejection of claims, 63
    deadline for responding, 62, 63
    extending response due deadline, 63
    need to avoid introduction of "new
        matter" in responding, 63
    response to, in patent application,
        62–67
    response must treat all issues raised
        in Office Action, 63
    submitting affidavits or other proofs
        in responding, 63
    substituting claims in responding, 63
    trademark, 137
Official Gazette, publication of issued
    patent data, 89
    publication of trademark for
        opposition, 137
Operativeness, as prerequisite for
    patentability, 41
Opposition, publication of trademark
    for, 137
Ornamentality requirement, 145

Parable of the Chair, 27–29
Paris Convention, 110
Partnership name registration, 5, 11

Pass, visitor, 93
Patent:
    applied for, 58, 59
    as contract, 25
    design, *see* Design patent
    file history, 67
    file issuance, 67
    misconceptions, 25–29
    notice of allowance, 61, 64, 67
    pending, 58, 59
    plant, *see* Plant patent
    program establishing procedures
        to protect important
        developments, 91–94
    reissue, *see* Reissue patent
    utility, *see* Utility patent
    value of, 31, 32
    why obtained, 29–31
Patentability, 33–45
    nonobviousness, 41–44
    novelty, 38, 41
    originality, 37, 38
    requirements in general, 34–35
    search, 46, 47
    statutory subject matter, 34–36
    utility, 34–41
Patentable subject matter, 33–45
Patent agent, 19
Patent applied for, definition, 58, 59
Patent attorney, 19
    compared with agent, 19
    directory, 19
    in-house, 21, 22
    selection, 19, 21
    services, 18, 19
    Yellow Pages listing, 19
Patent Cooperation Treaty, 111, 112
Patent pending, definition, 58, 59
Patent system:
    benefits of, 32
    constitutional basis, 32
    purpose of, 32
Patent and Trademark Office, 5, 6, 14,
    15
    applications, active, 6

processed into patents, 6
automation of, 6
Board of Appeals, 64
budget, 6
design patents issued by, 6
documents available for reference, 14, 15
documents missing or misfiled, 47
duty of candor in dealings with, 59, 60
employees, 6
examiners, 6
functions, 6
as library, 14, 15
location, 5, 6
papers filed daily, 6
plant patents issued by, 6
trademark registrations issued by, 6
utility patents issued by, 6
Pendency, time for applications, 6
Pending, applications, chain of, 69
patent, 6, 58, 59
Penicillin, consequences of failure to patent, 26, 27
Personal injury litigation and patents, 48
Petition for access to pending application, 59
Petition for extension to respond to office action, 63
Petty patent, 13
Phonograph records, copyright protection, 157
Plant patent, 10
number of patents issued, 6, 10
term, 10
Plant Variety Protection Act, 7
Principal Register, 134, 135
Printed matter unpatentable, 35
Prior art:
definition, 14
duty of candor with respect to, 59, 60
keeping abreast of, 14, 15
knowledge of, 14

Prior art statement, 60
Priority of invention, 81
Process, as statutory class of patentable subject matter, 34–36
Product:
definition, 34–36
fanciful features may acquire trademark significance, 129, 130
liability concerns considered in patent application, 48
look-alikes and trademark infringement, 128–130
of nature, 35
new use of old product patentable, 35
protecting configuration of, 128–130
redesign to avoid infringement, 48
Product-by-process claims, 52
Programs, computer patentability, 35
Property, intellectual, 3–5
Prosecution period, assignee intervention during, 104
Protest:
original application, 73
reissue application, 72, 73
Public Search Room, 14, 15, 47
documents misfiled or missing, 16, 17, 47
as library, 14, 15
limitations of, 47
paperless prototype planned, 17
searching in, 16, 17, 47
Publication:
definition of printed, 40
statutory bar, triggering act, 38–41
of trademark for opposition, 137
Publicity, right to, 3, 13

Quality control in trademark licensing, 141

"Reasonable examiner" test for selecting facts must be cited to PTO, 60

Reasons for allowance, examiner
    comments, 64, 65
  refuting reasons given by examiner,
    65
Record maintenance, 82–87
  conception documentation, 82
  diligence documentation, 86, 87
  disclosure format, 85, 86
  importance of witnesses, 82, 83
  invention notebook, 83–85
Redesign to avoid infringement, 89–91
Reduction to practice, 33
  actual, 33
  constructive, 33
Reexamination:
  of application after filing response,
    62–64
  of patent through reissue, 72, 73
Refund of excess fee payment, 57
Register:
  Principal, 134, 135
  Supplemental, 134, 135
Registration:
  copyright, 155, 156
  fictitious name, 11
  trademark, 133–139
  trade name, 11
Reinventing the wheel, 14
Reissue applications available for public
    inspection while pending, 59
Reissue patent:
  adversary participation in, 72, 73
  broadening, 72
  correction of defect by, 71, 72
  narrowing, 72
  reexamination by, 72, 73
Rejection of claims, 60–62, 64, 66, 67
  affidavits to overcome, 63
  double patenting, 66, 67
  final in patent prosecution, 64
Related company, control test in small
    entity status determination, 56,
    57
Release of invention rights by
    employer, 104

Renewal, trademark registration, 139
Representation by agent or attorney,
    14–21
Requirement:
  restriction, 65, 66
  species election, 65, 66
Response to office action, 62, 63
  form, 62
Restriction requirement, 62, 63
  request for reconsideration, 66
  traversing the requirement, 66
Right, negative character of patent
    grant, 27–29
Right to publicity, 3, 13
Royalty:
  intellectual property license, 107,
    141, 162
  patent license, 107
  trademark license, 141
  trade secret license, 162
Rule 75(e), 53

Safeguarding issued patent or
    trademark registration, 68
Sakraida v. AG. Pro. Inc., 43, 44
Sale, as statutory bar to patentability,
    44, 45
Saving provisions of copyright law, 158
Search:
  advantages stemming from, 14–17
  assignment, 18
  classes and subclasses, 14
  consultation with examiner, 16
  field of, 16
  index, 18
  infringement, 17, 18, 46
  limitations of, 47
  patentability, 46, 47
  state of art, 18
  team effort, 16, 17
  trademark availability, 123–127
  types of, 18
  validity, 18
Secondary considerations of
    nonobviousness, 43, 44

Secondary meaning, 148
Secrecy order, 36
Secrecy of pending applications, 59
Service mark, 10, 114
  example registration, Appendix III
Services, typical patent attorney, 18, 19
Settlement of patent suits, 78, 79
Shopright, 105
Show-how, 7, 12
Small entity status:
  defined, 56, 57
  fee reduction, 56, 57
  fraud in establishing, 57
  qualification for, 56, 57
Species election requirement, 65, 66
Specification, patent application, 48–50
  contents, 48–50
  description of preferred
    embodiment, 49
  summary of invention, 48–50
Statute of Monopolies, 32
Statutes:
  35 USC 101, 36
  35 USC 102, 38, 39, 44
  35 USC 102(a),(e),(g), 38, 40, 41
  35 USC 102(b),(c),(d), 44, 45
  35 USC 103, 39, 41–44
  35 USC 112, 51
  35 USC 261, 102
  35 USC 271, 77
  35 USC 286, 75
  35 USC 287, 70
  35 USC 289, 147
  35 USC 292, 71
Statutory bar, 38, 44, 45
Striking application from PTO files, 54
Sublicense provisions, 107, 108
Submitted ideas, agreements for
    handling, 96–98
Suggestive mark, 124, 125
Supplemental Register, 134, 135
Suppression of invention, 39, 41
Synergism, 43, 44

Taxes, annual maintenance, 55, 56, 110
Time extension, to respond to Office
    Action, 63
Trademark:
  abandonment, 126
  arbitrary, 124
  assignment, 140
  coined, 124, 126
  definition, 10, 11
  descriptive, 125
  duty to select mark posing no
    likelihood of confusion, 123, 124
  eligible subject matter, 121, 122
  enforcement of rights, 141, 142
  goodwill, 120, 121
  incontestibility of registration, 138, 139
  infringement, 141, 142
  licensing, 141
  likelihood of confusion, test of
    infringement, 123, 124
  maintaining files of specimens, 131, 132
  number of active registrations, 6, 10
  number of applications filed, 6, 11
  number of registrations issued, 6
  opposition, 137, 138
  proper use of, 128–130
  publication for opposition, 137, 138
  quality control in licensing, 141
  registration:
    examples of, Appendix Three
    procedure, 133–139
    symbol, 128
  relationship to copyrights, 119, 120
  relationship to design patents, 148, 149
  relationship to monoplies, 117, 118
  relationship to names, 117
  relationship to patents, 119
  relationship to unfair competition, 117–119
  renewal of registration, 139
  secondary meaning, 148
  selection of, 123–127

Trademark (*Continued*)
  state registration of, 135, 136
  strength of, 124–126
  suggestive, 124, 125
  symbols used with, 128
  time of pendency of application, 6
  types of, 120, 124, 125
  unprotectable terms, 125
  "use" as essential element, 122
Trademark attorney, 19
Trade name, 11
  definition, 11
  relationship to trademarks, 120
  state registration of, 5, 11
Trade secret, 7, 12, 160–164
  advantages, 162
  bases of protection, 162, 163
  definition, 12
  disadvantages, 162
  elements of, 160
  employee agreements concerning,
    163, 164
  guarding, 163
  loss of, 162
  protecting secrecy of, 163
  relationship to patents, 161, 162
Traversing election requirement, 66

Unfair competition, relationship to
  trademarks, 117
Uniformity in patent-related decision,
  77, 78
Unpublished work, copyright
  protection, 152, 159
Use:
  experimental, 40, 45
  public as statutory bar to
    patentability, 39, 40, 44, 45
Useful arts, 34, 41
Utility, as prerequisite for
  patentability, 34, 41
Utility Model Registration, 13
Utility patent:
  allowance, 64, 67
  application amendment, 62, 63

application content, 48–50
applied for, 58, 59
best mode requirement of
  applications, 50, 51
claim amendment, 62–64
claim format, 52, 53
correction of defects, 71
correction of errors, 67, 68, 71
declaration, 53, 54
defensive use of, 79, 80
definition, 7, 8
description requirement of
  application, 50, 51
design, *see* Design patent
distinctness requirement of
  application, 50, 51
duty of candor in prosecution, 59,
  60
enablement requirement of
  application, 50, 51
enforcement, 74–81
error correction, 67, 68, 71
examination of, 60–67
example of, Appendix One
execution, 53, 54
Express Mail filing, 57
fees, 55–57
marking, 58, 59, 70, 71
misuse, 76, 77
monopoly misconceptions, 26
negative right granted by, 27–29
notice of allowance, 61, 64, 67
number of applications filed, 6, 8
number of patents issued, 6
pending, 6, 58, 59
petty, 13
prosecution, 58–69
reasons for allowance, examiner
  comments on, 64, 65
relationship to copyrights, 147
relationship to trademarks, 148,
  149
relationship to trade secrets, 152
safeguarding original document, 68
secrecy of pending applications, 59

settling suit, 78, 79
small entity status, 56, 57
term, 7, 8
time of pendency of application, 6
value of, 31, 32

Validity:
opinion from Patent and Trademark
Office through reissue, 72, 73
search, 18

Value of patent, 31, 32
Visitor passes, 92, 93

Work for hire, 154
Working requirement of foreign patent
laws, 110
Works of art, protection of, 152, 153

Yellow Pages, attorney listing, 19